ALSO BY HARRY REASONER

Tell Me About Women (a novel)

The Reasoner Report (collected broadcast pieces)

BEFORE
THE COLORS
FADE

BEFORE
THE COLORS
FADE

By Harry Reasoner

ALFRED A. KNOPF   *New York*   1981

Library of Congress Cataloging in Publication Data
Reasoner, Harry, [*date*]
Before the colors fade.

1. Reasoner, Harry [*date*].   2. Journalists—
United States—Biography.   3. Television broadcasting
of news—United States.   I. Title.
PN4874.R34A33   1981   070'.92'4   [B].   81-47490
ISBN 0-394-50480-1   AACR2

Manufactured in the United States of America

Published October 1, 1981
Reprinted Once
Third Printing, October 1981

To Don Hewitt

See page 157

Contents

Contents

BEFORE
THE COLORS
FADE

Introduction

I AM THE CORRESPONDENT who worked for both Fred Friendly and Roone Arledge, which is a little bit like having served under both Napoleon *and* Custer. I came east in the summer of 1956 to join CBS News, spent seven and a half years at ABC, and in the fall of 1981 I am back with CBS News. At this point in time, to steal a phrase from John Dean, I am still working, still, by most medical standards, reasonably non-senile. I have done and can do every job in television news except to be an executive like Friendly or Arledge, and I came close to that once. I have interviewed Orval Faubus and Leila Khaled, the Palestinian terrorist, and the Duke of Windsor, and an obnoxious Indian named Krishna Menon. I knew Dwight Eisenhower and Lyndon Johnson well, John Kennedy not well, and Richard Nixon as well as I wanted to.

Those random notes are intended to be like the opening

statement an expert witness gives in a trial, to establish his credentials to talk about something. What I want to talk about is the first twenty-five years of television news, or at least my first twenty-five years in television news, which is approximately the same thing. That is my starting point, that I was there when it began and watched what happened.

This is not a history of television news, and it is not quite autobiography either. It is an attempt instead to get some of this down before it quite becomes history. Twenty-five years of my one lifetime span the infancy, the precocious and generally beloved childhood, the troubled and besieged youth, and what is perhaps the premature old age of my profession, or craft, or racket. It should be useful to mine my own memory before all this subsides into something to be excavated by academics.

Some of us came into the craft—as you see, I think of "craft" rather than either "profession" or "racket"—very early, and we formed it. We had to. Before the network news program began to stretch and feel and learn in the middle 1950's, no one had ever done news with moving pictures before. America was used to newsreels—the little stories with music, the annual sheep-shearing competitions, the fashion shows and White House Easter Egg rolls and Lew Lehr noting that monkeys are the craziest people. Newsreels didn't cover news: there was a feeling that people didn't want news when they went to the movies.

In the late fifties Gordon Yoder of Texas, who was beginning to shoot news film for ABC, carried two cameras with him. He had a bulky 35-millimeter Bell & Howell that used film rolls lasting only about a minute, for what was left of his employer's newsreel clients, and he had a neater 16-millimeter Filmo for the network. The idea was that if any assignment offered a newsreel possibility, he would get out the big camera and shoot it. But he knew his customers —and in the great and blazing stories in Little Rock and Montgomery, where I knew him, he never took the newsreel camera out of its box. Filmmakers had never dealt with news.

A dozen or so people in New York and on the road had to figure out how to change all that, how to use film to report news events for daily broadcasts, how to edit it, how to get it on the air. Don Hewitt at CBS was inventing the two-projector system, which eliminated three days to three weeks of the steps that documentary producers had to live with. Hewitt put one piece of edited film on one projector, one on another. As they clicked along, he would take what he wanted—picture from one, sound from another, and make a kind of evanescent electronic meld on the outgoing television signal. Since there was no videotape, what he created never actually existed except as the passing image that you saw, and if he used such a story on the 6:45 edition of the evening news, he had to work the same magic all over again on the 7:15 edition. It required a director and film editors and control-room technical directors who possessed sensitivity and a kind of choreographic rhythm. They had that. Two-, three-, and four-projector stories, carefully melded ahead of time on videotape, are now so routine that most people putting them together think the system has been around forever.

In the field, reporters who were the film industry's first

journalists were figuring how to give Don Hewitt and his colleagues what they needed. People like Phil Scheffler and Bob Allison and Charles Kuralt at CBS, people like Sandy Vanocur and John Chancellor at NBC. They—and, all right, I—were the first reporters in broadcast news to come out of film and television, not from radio news or the Korean War or World War II. And we weren't the "contact reporters" who worked with newsreel cameramen to get the names spelled right for a caption sheet.

I wish I could write about them all—the cameramen and the soundmen and the electricians. Carlo, the elegant soundman from Rome who, it turned out in an improbable restaurant in Niamey, in Niger at the edge of Africa's Saharan famine belt, could speak a little Vietnamese. Joe Dalisera, a soundman of incredible courtesy and cheer. Jerry Slattery, the profession's favorite electrician. The mention of Joe, incidentally, reminds us that in between the laughs and the long boredoms and the competitions, this is a craft that can kill. He died in a helicopter crash in late 1980. It was a story which involved getting film from an island in the Bahamas to Miami every night; as he of course would, Joe had volunteered to be the courier. The weather was marginal; the helicopter just disappeared. God rest his soul. And all the cameramen. Al Gretz, dead now, with whom I did my first good network story in the winter of 1956. Don Norling, cool and meticulous in the middle of Little Rock's riots. And Wendell Hoffman and Mario Biasetti and Laurens Pierce. Some of them, and others, will pop up in the pages to come. They deserve to. A lot of the pioneering correspondents got to be pretty well known, but only rarely does a cameraman get a mention. And yet they had to be as innovative and journalistically informed as the reporters—and in addition they had to keep their cameras clean and remember to follow focus and deal with primitive and balky equipment. They made us look good, and when the day was done and the reporters went to dinner, the cameramen put the film in cans and worried about how to ship it and charged batteries and repacked.

This, I hope, is the story of how things grew. I don't suppose we thought much about what we were doing, how we were forming the habits and the principles and the techniques and the morals of our craft. It's just as well; the sense of responsibility might have immobilized us. It was only a couple of years later that Don Hewitt was able to put a little sign on the screen at the end of the program called *Douglas Edwards with the News.* The sign said: "More people get their news from this CBS broadcast than from any other single source in the world." How all that came about and how well we reared this infant is worth remembering, before the colors fade.

I SUPPOSE I SHOULD ELABORATE on my first sentence, first, because there may be a lot of you out there who neither know nor care who Fred Friendly and Roone Arledge are, and, second, because if I lump Fred Friendly with Roone Arledge without elaboration, Mr. Friendly will have a set of kittens. So: Fred Friendly has been one of the great movers and shakers of this craft—Edward R. Murrow's producer, president of CBS News, dispenser of philosophy and funds for the Ford Foundation. There will be more about him later. Roone Arledge was the flamboyant producer who made a great success out of ABC Sports and in 1977 became also president of ABC News. It seems likely that at that point he was in over his head.

What these two men have in common is the attribute of great natural force; those whose lives they have touched were frequently never quite the same again. Fred once hired a new assistant, and after a few months of the kind of days Fred put people through, the assistant, his wife, and Fred were all at the same cocktail party.

"If we don't get some order into our lives," said the wife, "I'm going to explode. I'll get a divorce."

"Oh, come on, Edna," said the assistant, "it isn't that bad."

"It's that bad," she said. "If Fred doesn't ease up on you, I'm going to get a divorce."

"I can live with that," said Fred.

1

Background

As P. G. Wodehouse once noted, the great problem with beginning a story is to decide how much background you have to put in before getting in the swing of it. I will be brief. I got into television news at the age of thirty-one, in late 1954. At the time I had not really been a practicing reporter for six years, since the newspaper I worked for in Minneapolis faltered, slipped and fell, and had to be destroyed. I had spent a couple of years, pleasantly enough, as a public-relations man; I had written news for a radio station, and I had served three years in the Far East as an officer of the United States Information Agency. I had, depending on your analysis, either been drifting or getting well rounded.

We—my wife, Kay, and I and the children—enjoyed the time in Manila. But midway through the tour we played bridge one night with the senior career officer at the Embassy, a man in his late forties with five children, a man holding the top permanent Foreign Service rank. He mentioned casually that a milestone was coming up for him: his oldest child was ready for college and he had that morning arranged a loan for the first year's tuition and expenses.

This seemed to us to say something about government service as a career. If a man who had spent twenty years working for the government, a man who had attained top rank and pay, had to borrow money to send a child to college, there was something wrong. We agreed that the Foreign Service, with all its rewards, was something to get out of. So, on home leave, I looked for a job in New York. No one offered me one, but Sig Mickelson, then president of CBS News, who had been a teacher of mine at the University of Minnesota, said that if I would go out and get some experience, he might give me a chance.

I got the experience at a station then called KEYD-TV, in Minneapolis. It was an independent station, locally owned, just opening with great plans for local programming and public service. I became news director. I was the news *department*, as a matter of fact, except for the part-time services of the station's one film cameraman, who also shot commercials. We did a news broadcast at six o'clock in the evening, another one at ten o'clock, and after a while cameraman Bill Knoll and I also produced a half-hour weekly documentary of a sort. One was a half-hour film about race prejudice in Minneapolis (that was a novel idea in 1955); we entered it in a competition for the Robert E. Sherwood Awards. There were only two prizes for local stations in the awards, first place and runner-up. First place got $25,000. Runner-up got a certificate. We were runner-up.

We never had much of an audience. In those early days the dominance of the networks over local audiences was even greater—probably much greater—than it is now, and our entry as the fourth station in the Twin Cities market didn't make much impression. We got high ratings, as a station, on only two occasions, as I remember it. Once was when we carried the state high-school basketball tournament. And once was when Adlai Stevenson came to town for a political speech and the Democratic Party bought a half-hour, for simultaneous use, on all three network stations. The theory was that people would have to listen to Mr. Stevenson, since they had no choice. Well, they did have a choice—us, Channel 9—and they turned to it in droves, giving us our highest non-sports audience in our brief history. We were showing, as I recall it, a Red Cross film on water safety. It didn't make me cynical about the preferences of the average American viewer, for two reasons: I was already aware that people will do almost anything to avoid listening to a political speech, and, second, I tend to agree with them. Of course, as adroit a speaker as Adlai Stevenson versus a film on water safety might give you pause. But there is a lot of water in Minnesota and I suppose people were concerned about it.

We put on a good deal of programming like water safety, and fourth re-runs of a syndicated show called *My Little Margie*, and re-runs of some very strange old movies, with an announcer sitting in an easy chair and, during the frequent interruptions of the film, introducing commercials about Preparation H and the Leader Furniture Store and cold remedies. It was before the days of Contac and Oil of Olay, or we might have made it.

A note on those old movies: Our nightly movie was called Tower Theater, I think, but among the staff we called it Cuemark Theater. You must have noticed, to this day, the occasional round bleep of light in the upper-right-hand corner of the screen during a movie; that warns technicians and announcers that a commercial interval is coming up in ten seconds. You make it, I suppose, by just scratching away a bit of the picture in a few frames. The trouble is that then —and now—the movies that make the rounds of the independent stations get a lot of cuemarks on them, since a lot of stations want their commercial intervals at different times, or maybe more of them. (In that case harried local film programmers frequently just chop out ten minutes of the film here and there; they don't have time to look at the story. This produces some weird plot developments and I like to think keeps the audience on its toes.) So an old popular film that has been around will have so many cuemarks on it that even the most alert technician has trouble recognizing his, and for the viewer it is like a continual halation in the right-hand corner. It is sometimes more interesting than the film.

Anyhow, it was a good place to learn about television, because when I did something badly, there weren't many people out there to notice. And I had the freedom to invent and improvise and be not only reporter but writer and producer. The weekly documentary was an example: it was called *Twin City Heartbeat* and it was chartered to show people worthwhile institutions in the Twin Cities. We did Hennepin County General Hospital and the Girl Scouts and the public library; and we learned how to do what we wanted inside our budget, which was $300 a show. (The budget for a similar local show on a good station these days would be at least ten times that, maybe twenty.) We wanted to do dialogues between people, but the simple fact was that we didn't get enough of Bill Knoll's time to shoot sound, and we had no practical way to edit it if we did. So I thought I invented something. In a conversation on location, we would record the voices on an audio tape recorder, which is easy to edit. But we would film with an easy silent camera the person who *wasn't* talking. That meant the dialogue, as edited, didn't have to be in synchronization with the people speaking. It would have looked a little odd to a professional, but it worked. As noted, I invented it. There were probably a lot of people in similar situations inventing it at the same time. That's the way television grew: improvising to meet a need, and then institutionalizing it. If Don Hewitt hadn't invented the two-projector system, someone else would have, maybe.

We also invented a couple of things which would be questioned, I suspect, at CBS. For example, in our story on the local general hospital, the most attractive character was a student nurse. But she was relatively inarticulate and froze on camera. So after talking to her a good deal about her life, I wrote a narration for her in the first person, and she recorded it on audio tape, which didn't bother her, and we laid it over beautiful silent pictures of her going about her duties (Bill Knoll was an exceptionally talented photographer). It was a little like docu-dramas of the present day, but it worked. It was better.

I say later on that I began writing little end-pieces on the Saturday- and then Sunday-night news broadcasts in New York, but actually I started in Minneapolis. These got some attention from our dozens of viewers, and stuck in my mind as a legitimate way for a broadcaster to say something personal. Here's one, as reprinted by *Minneapolis Tribune* columnist Will Jones—the fact that Jones was a friend of mine I'm sure was irrelevant in his decision to reprint it:

> You may remember that last week on our inside story of the Margaret-Townsend romance we predicted there would be no marriage. We are now able to tell you exclusively why, from the same drunken sailor who gave us the other inside story.
>
> It's because of Elsa Maxwell. Margaret, considering the thing from all angles, has made a fairly deep study of the married life of her Uncle Edward, who gave up the throne for a woman named Wallis.
>
> Margaret could probably foresee herself and Capt. Townsend in a few years, when the glamor of a daring marriage had worn off, when her face had begun to sag like Wallis's, and when Capt. Townsend, his waistline gone, had let his membership expire in the Gentlemen Jockeys club. She could probably foresee those gay parties at which she and an aging Uncle Edward might stare at each other with the same inexpressible boredom you can see in his eyes now in news pictures.

> Better spinsterhood and a box of souvenirs tied
> up in a lavender ribbon, Margaret decided, than
> marriage and a string of parties with Elsa Maxwell
> and her lavender friends.

This is the kind of year it was: by the end of the first year of operation, the high-minded local businessmen who owned KEYD were tired of losing money, and three things happened in rapid succession. Our news department was named the best in the five-state Northwest area, the businessmen sold the station, and the new owners told us they were going to dispense with the news department.

But I had the experience Sig Mickelson had advised me to get, and I had a good deal of confidence. Some very good journalists never feel at home in television, but I had felt comfortable from the first in this strange land. I wrote Sig and told him I was ready.

The reply was from John Day, Sig's director of news. It offered me a job as a summer replacement on the assignment desk. The employment would be guaranteed only for nineteen weeks; the salary would be $157.50 a week. There would be no allowance for moving expenses. I had been making twice that; to move to New York for a fifty-percent cut in salary seemed insane. I wrote Mr. Day and declined. Then, a week or so later, I had a conversation with my wife. I would be the first to admit that she has her faults, but she also had a knack, at moments of crisis, for seeing an issue clearly and courageously. "You'd better go," she said. "I don't want you spending your forties blaming me and the children for keeping you from your chance in the big time."

I called CBS the next day and the job was still open. I kissed everybody goodbye and got on a train and went east.

Incidentally, the next time I had an offer to take a fifty-percent cut in salary was twenty-two years later, when CBS offered to bring me home from ABC. Again, I took it. I have a Scotsman's instinct in these matters.

I SUPPOSE THE SUMMER OF 1956, when I began work at CBS News, was an innocent interlude in the history of the United States after World War II. We had had problems in the United States Information Agency with the influence of Senator Joseph McCarthy, whose activities back home had put the country into a kind of paranoid anti-communism. USIA libraries were checked to make sure there were no books which McCarthy's traveling agents could find suspect; the propaganda materials we published were simplistically pure. But the worst of that had passed by 1956. The war in Korea was over. The French war in Vietnam was over and the disintegration of the government in South Vietnam that seduced us into war had not yet gotten serious. Dwight Eisenhower was about to be renominated and re-elected.

I think I know how most people felt in 1956: they felt that just possibly the American dream *would* work forever. There must have been signs then of a deteriorating environment, but nobody was paying attention. There certainly were signs of the developing revolution in expectations of black citizens, but not many people were paying attention. There were probably even signs of the failure of a successful materialistic society to produce happy, cheerful, healthy children, but those signs would have been obscure. The children and young people that you saw and heard in those days appeared to be happy, indeed jolly creatures. They were pushing a little against the moral strictures of their parents, but in a lovable, precocious way, like the characters in a pre-war Andy Hardy movie. They were with apparent enthusiasm engaging in the kind of youthful and organized wildnesses which so quickly—in the seventies—became in softened outline the subject of nostalgia for the later decade's children.

It was the same with the adults. It was an era where people believed that it was quite possible for everyone to be prosperous and buy a Charmglow gaslight for the front walk that ran between the trim lawns where all the mosquitoes had been killed by DDT. There was an Eisenhower recession in the offing, but there was the Eisenhower happiness at hand. The President played golf in the afternoons and most people thought that was fine. His Vice President talked about the dangers of communism and Democratic softness, but there was none of the sense of urgency and peril of the days of Josef Stalin. The new cars came in two tones and sometimes three and had big tailfins which were believed to stabilize your motion at speeds of over seventy. The bigger cars got eight and ten and twelve miles to the gallon, but that was all right. The idea of a government agency issuing mileage figures for cars would have seemed novel indeed; not even Adlai Stevenson had thought of it. No one had ever heard of Ralph Nader or Stokely Carmichael or Patricia Hearst.

This situation, this brief Era of Good Feeling, was what

CBS News was covering when I joined it. The big stories that summer, up to the time of the political conventions, were not connected with big issues. The Monday that I reported for work at the end of July, the lead story on *Douglas Edwards with the News* was still the sinking of the *Andrea Doria*. The previous week Doug and Don Hewitt had made history, flying over the wreck while Doug described the scene the camera was recording. I say "made history," and that probably needs a bit of explanation. There had been moving pictures of burning or sinking boats before—at least as early as the *Normandie*, gutted in the Hudson River in World War II. But I think this was the first time the reporter and the camera were both on the scene, both dealing with a news event, not a curiosity or a piece of history, for use on television *that* day. Phil Scheffler, the senior man on the assignment desk, was in Parris Island, South Carolina, covering the trial of a Marine sergeant who had led a night patrol of recruits into a swamp, with ensuing deaths. In New York the major local story was a kidnapping. There were, I think, seven men on the assignment desk. They were all men, and they were all white.

Not to be teleological, this period of desultory news may have been fortunate, a training period for what was to come. Stumblingly, we were developing the technology and the techniques for what lay ahead.

In THOSE DAYS the assignment desk at CBS News was different and probably more important than it became later. The reason was that the men on the desk then not only kept track of the news and made assignments, just as the name said, but they also were the reporters who, increasingly, went out to cover the stories. It happened in this way: At first, almost all film stories were silent film. Sometimes there was some natural sound or the voice of the subject of the story talking, but mostly it was just silent film, shot by some per-diem free-lancer in Toledo or Miami or Dallas and flown to Washington or New York for processing and use. If it went to Washington, a correspondent named Neil Strawser looked at it, directed its editing, and wrote a script for it. He then read the script, live, from an announcer's booth as the film was fitted into the evening news. He did this at 6:45 Eastern time and again at 7:15 Eastern time—the two times from which affiliated stations could choose to carry the broadcast. If the film went to Chicago, the same process was in the hands of Frank Reynolds. Neil is still a CBS News correspondent; Frank, at this writing, is the senior anchor of ABC News. But at that time there were a lot of editions of *Douglas Edwards with the News* where the only voices you heard, besides Doug's, were Neil's and Frank's.

It soon became apparent, as Don Hewitt and the others became more familiar with and confident about their new craft, that there would be major advantages to having a reporter on the scene *reporting*, that if television news was going to be different from and better than the newsreels, the reporter, rather than the cameraman, would have to be responsible for the editorial content and direction of the story. There should be a reporter saying things and illuminating what the camera showed. So the assignment desk began to send its men out on stories: down the street for a couple of hours to interview Nelson Rockefeller, or for a week at a time to the Parris Island trial.

Why send these unknown young men from the assignment desk out on the stories when CBS News was staffed by people like Charles Collingwood and Alexander Kendrick and George Herman? There were at least three reasons. First, those names were usually not available—they were overseas, or they had regular radio assignments, or they were tied up with Murrow and Friendly in documentary work. The new and struggling evening news was still to some extent a stepchild, and treated as such. Second, both executives and correspondents, trained and steeped in the glamor and prestige of CBS Radio, were a little reluctant to exchange the familiar and assured precincts of radio for the new medium. An assignment for the evening news frequently meant spending two or three days with an unsympathetic cameraman whose unreliable equipment could make the whole day a frustration; bringing in the several thousand feet of film to New York for editing; and, if the laboratory didn't ruin the film, seeing the final result as a minute-and-a-half story on a broadcast that as yet didn't have half the audience of radio's *World News Roundup* or *The World Tonight*.

But the most important reason was that this new kind of reporting needed a new kind of reporter, an agile and durable fellow who knew and liked film, who knew and understood what Don Hewitt wanted, who felt at home in a ninety-second report. The new kind: Reasoner, Scheffler, Jaffe, Karasik, Allison, Schakne, Costigan, and, before long, a writer from the Edwards show named Kuralt. These were names that even most of the people at CBS didn't know. We were not the aristocrats of journalism like the great names of CBS Radio. We were not even in a journalism fraternity—we were members of IATSE, the International Alliance of Theatrical Stage Employees, the cameramen's union, and we were technically called reporter-contacts. We were, in relation to the august company of correspondents, enlisted men or, at best, warrant officers.

As specified by IATSE, our pay was $157.50 for a forty-hour week. But not really a forty-hour week. In a concession to the sometimes long travel days and erratic manpower requirements of news coverage, the union accepted a seven-week, 280-hour cycle. Overtime, which we all counted on, was paid on that basis. Thus, in theory, if the man who kept track of that sort of thing noticed that Scheffler, five weeks into a cycle, had already accumulated 282 hours of working time, and if the news was temporarily quiet, he could "knock off" Scheffler for a week—give him the time involuntarily off—and save the company forty hours of time-and-a-half pay. It became a contest for us to prevent that sort of disaster. Once I was ending a sixth week with sixty-eight hours of overtime already and I badly wanted the other forty. But things were slow, I could feel the chill breath of the knock-off on my neck. I went to James Burke, who as managing editor was one of my bosses, and pointed out that I had vacation time coming and asked for a week of it to begin on Monday. Mild and pleasant and aware that it was a quiet time, he approved. I went home, and, sure enough, at dinnertime came a call from Frank Donghi, who as national editor was responsible for the hours and overtime of the reporters.

"Take next week off," said Frank, "you're knocked off."

"I'm sorry, Frank," I said, "I'm on vacation next week."

"Oh, shit," he said.

It was a nice little petty triumph. But the overtime and the long days enabled us to make a good deal more than $157.50 a week. As a matter of fact, when I became a correspondent, working on a contract which specified a base salary against fees for each appearance on the air and had no overtime provisions, my income for the first full year was around $12,000—a couple of hundred dollars less than I had made in my last full year as a lowly reporter-contact. Things got better, though.

As it had become clear that daily television news needed reporters, it also became clear that as the evening news broadcast became more widely watched, produced with more sophistication—became more important—the highly visible reporter could not very well be a junior union technician. There were here two choices, and the natural inclination was to try one of them first: use the better-known names, the more mature reporters from radio and documentaries, but send along with one of these veterans a kid from the assignment desk to handle the prosaic matters of telling the cameraman what to shoot, of preparing a script that complemented rather than fought the film, of finding lodging and coffee and amusement for the correspondent. I think all of us on the desk did that several times: I went to Lake Charles, Louisiana, to help Doug Edwards report on a hurricane, and I went to Galveston to assist Bill Downs in the coverage of an important convention of the Teamsters' union. Bill Downs, who died in 1978, was easy to help. He knew more about the reporting than I did, and my job was only to help him fit it into a film format. I remember that trip for another reason. It was the convention in which the Teamsters decided to drop their president, Dave Beck, who was in trouble with the law. The man behind the decision seemed to be a fellow named Jimmy Hoffa, who already had quite a reputation for toughness. The surprise was to find Hoffa had a definite, rough charm. He stopped in a hall one day to shoot dice with several of the reporters. I won $7.50.

There was nothing undignified in this. We were, mostly, younger and, if not younger, certainly junior to the men we assisted. As things developed, several of the assignment-desk men stayed in this role, creating another new division of our craft: the field producer. Phil Scheffler did that, for instance. But for some of us—myself, I know, and I'd guess Charles Kuralt—there was a major question of ego. We had grown up with a kind of mystical feeling about the title "CBS News Correspondent," and we wanted to be a CBS News Correspondent. Good Lord, that was *Murrow's* title. Other journalists on newspapers were reporters; reporters who worked for CBS News were correspondents.

I don't know what the executives were thinking. But I do know that in the early winter of 1957 I was called from the ratty and depressing quarters of television news in the old Grand Central Building to the home building of all of CBS at 485 Madison Avenue, where radio news operated, where Murrow had his office, and where the executives lived. John Day wanted to see me. I thought I knew why. CBS had a Sunday-afternoon program then, a sort of news of the week in review, and it had been widely reported that one of the reporter-contacts was going to be detached from the desk and assigned to that program full time. It was believed it would be an interesting and profitable assignment—lots of travel, lots of overtime—but it would not be *the* promotion that someone had to get sometime.

What John Day wanted to tell me was that I was being named a CBS News Correspondent—the first to be named out of television news. The same title as Edward R. Murrow and Howard K. Smith.

I walked out onto Madison Avenue in as impervious a state of euphoria as I have ever known. Excluding personal matters like wedding days and births of children, it was and has continued to be the biggest day of my life.

2

How It Was

So I was a CBS News Correspondent. I left IATSE with an honorable-withdrawal card and joined AFTRA—the American Federation of Television and Radio Artists. I worked on a contract, with no overtime. It paid, as I recall, a base salary of $175 a week plus $75 a week advance and guarantee against fees. The fee system has mostly disappeared by now—to the good, I guess. It would probably be impossible to operate today's huge news departments, with the concomitant situations of reporters and correspondents plugging away at necessary things but not getting on the air all that often, on the fee system. But at that time all the correspondents were on fees. It took me only a little while to realize why most of the correspondents, all of whom were senior to me, thought the fee system was the greatest invention since the wheel, and only a little longer to realize why that judgment wasn't true in my case.

The way it worked was like this: if you appeared, or your voice was used, in a network news broadcast, you were credited with $50 against your fee advance, less a mysterious twenty percent which was deducted for credit against your basic salary. If you made a report for radio news, you got $25. If you actually handled a radio news broadcast, which I didn't in those days, you got a larger fee—it may have been $75. And, of course, if you were *Douglas Edwards with the News* or Walter Cronkite with *Sunday News Special*, or if you were the host of *Face the Nation* or regularly assigned to the local news broadcasts in New York, you got regular and larger fees. The largest fee in television news at CBS at that time was Cronkite's for the *Sunday News*. The understanding was that Walter—busy with programs like *You Are There* and *The Twentieth Century* and a daily ten-minute broadcast at one o'clock in the afternoon—had not wanted to be the anchor on the experimental Sunday-night broadcast, but they had wanted him badly and had finally persuaded him with a very large fee (for 1960) and for a fifteen-minute newscast. He got $600 for it, and so did people who substituted for him, and so did I when he moved on to the weekday evening news and the *Sunday News* became mine in 1962. It was very nice, but a measure of how long radio had been around and how new was television was the fact that the *Sunday News* fee was not the biggest fee in all of CBS News. That distinction belonged to a radio news broadcast: *Lowell Thomas and the News*. Lowell got, and in terms of audience still earned, $800 a night, five nights a week, and so did the people who substituted for him. I never did.

The trouble with this lovely system was that I didn't have any of the regular assignments or sinecures which guaranteed the big paycheck. Occasionally, in Cuba or Little Rock or somewhere, I would get a flurry of radio assignments, but basically what I did was TV news and features for *Douglas Edwards with the News*. You could spend a week on an assignment, working with the primitive Auricon camera and with optical sound recording. With optical sound and with film you did not know until you got back and the film went to the laboratory whether you had an image on the film, or whether the funny little wobbly light-track that ran down the side of single-system film would actually reproduce the sounds you had heard when it was struck by the beamed light in the projector. You could work a week, in other words, and find out on the following Monday that you might as well have stayed in bed.

Or even if you had a lucky week and got two stories on the evening news and made two reports for radio, you had to wait awhile to count your chickens. That was because the fiends in the business-affairs department had this little joker in your contract: the $75-a-week advance and guarantee on fees was based on a thirteen-week cycle. You could make $150, less that damned twenty percent, in fees one week; the following week the laboratory could ruin all the film you had brought back from a hazardous flight with the Navy's early-warning radar planes from Newfoundland to the Azores, and you were back $20 in the hole on that thirteen-week cycle. I had the same *title* as Murrow and Smith and all those fellows, but I lived in a barn in Connecticut and turned in insurance policies for their cash value, and my kids, I think, were vaguely aware that, compared to most of the commuters who lived in Westport and Weston, we were fairly poor. They also, I think, felt that in some way their father couldn't get a good job like the other fathers, who were home for Little League and picnics and school concerts while he was always packing a bag and leaving for the airport at nine o'clock at night, or gone weekends, or simply groggy.

I LOVED IT. I would have loved it more, I suppose, if there had been more money, or if I had been a bachelor, or if things had been better organized at home so that, finishing a story in New Orleans at eight o'clock at night, I could have had a luxurious sleep-in instead of catching an eleven-o'clock plane in a thunderstorm to get to Connecticut and salve my conscience at having left a partner stuck with five, and then six, small children, and all the work and not enough money to move loosely. But with all of it, I loved it.

It would be like this: I would catch the 4:30 train to Connecticut after a hot and useless day in the office; no news anywhere in the world needing a correspondent from New York, no enthusiasm for doing expense accounts, a desultory day and a heavy lunch and dozing on the dirty train, and then the drive home from the station in the $50 1947 Hudson I had acquired as a second car. It was kind of an attractive car: two tones of an off-blue and a luxury look if you didn't notice that the left rear door was tied shut and that the muffler was wired to the rear bumper. It had only one real peculiarity: its starter didn't work at all. This was no problem at home—the driveway was relatively steeply slanted, and all I had to do was to park facing downhill and start it in gear. But at the station I had to find a parking place on an incline and back into it. The system worked. Only twice in the year or so that I used the Hudson for a station car did I have to get a push.

So I would get home—or, to get out of this morass of the subjunctive and tell the story of one particular event, I got home. I made a drink for self and spouse and sat in the kitchen, or maybe we all walked down the hill to the pond and splashed a bit in the forgiving evening light of Daylight Saving Time, and then we ate dinner. We made as much of a thing as we could of everyone—seven or eight of us by then—eating at the same time if I was home. I don't know when that began to erode, but I suspect the surest sign of family disintegration is when you don't have the evening meal together.

And at eight o'clock the telephone rang, and it was the assignment desk. The United States Air Force had managed to drop an atomic bomb in a farmyard in Florence, South Carolina. They were being nonchalant about it; there had never been a possibility that the nuclear warhead on the bomb would explode, the Air Force explained, and the inadvertent dropping of the bomb from the practicing aircraft was a one-in-a-billion chance that would never be repeated. But the conventional explosive charge designed to detonate the atomic material in a for-real case *had* gone off on impact, digging quite a hole in the farmyard, and the citizens of Florence and state authorities and a lot of other worriers were considerably exercised.

The efficient assignment desk had done most of my preliminary work for me. They had determined that I could get a plane from La Guardia late that night to somewhere—Greenville, maybe—catch a little sleep, and meet Wendell Hoffman, the cameraman. They had arranged for a charter to Florence in the morning. If Wendell and I got the story by noon, we could charter back to Greenville and catch a commercial flight to Washington. With any luck at all, we could develop, edit, and script the film in time for the evening news.

The surprising things about those days was that usually it all worked, sort of. There was indeed a plane at La Guardia, and I made it, and when I got to the rendezvous point and went to the motel, there was a message saying Wendell would indeed arrive by morning.

I should digress briefly about Wendell. In those days when I played fireman out of New York, I worked with him more than any other one man. We went to Cuba twice during Batista's last days, we went to a revolution in Panama that we couldn't find, we went to Galveston and New Orleans and Udall, Kansas, and we spent a lot of time in Little Rock.

Wendell was a little older than I was, and it occurs to me now in surprise that I don't know how he got to be a cameraman. He was a Nebraska boy and a farmer by avocation, but in the years we worked together he lived in Manhattan, Kansas, and he was one of maybe three or four cameramen of choice for the quick story, the nighttime flight, the charter, the impossible deadline. He had been the man who walked with seventy pounds of camera equipment into the Sierra Maestra to get the first film interview with Fidel Castro, and then carried it down again and got it out of Cuba, and then went back with me to frolic in the more comfortable but sinister and conspiratorial night clubs and back streets and restaurants of the last days of capitalistic Havana. I suspect he was more comfortable in the Sierra Maestra: more than any other cameraman I've ever known, he got involved in stories. A picture in my mind of him is at an interview. He had gotten the camera running and aimed right, and then I became conscious that as the questions and the answers heated up, he was gradually edging out from behind the camera and toward me and the subject. It obviously took a lot of self-discipline for him not to join the questioning; something inside him that he would not admit the existence of told him that he could probably ask better questions, and he may well have been able to.

He was a tall man of substantial intelligence who had retained the voice and mannerisms of the midwestern farm-land (I am not being patronizing, so had I). He had faced more personal tragedies, and continued to in the years ahead, than any one man is entitled to, and they hurt him, but they never affected his meticulous and beautiful work. He had that rare and lovely combination of great courage and considerable strength mixed with courtesy and gentleness, and even when he had to work with some of the slobs in the business he never whined or blamed them.

For the kind of story we were headed for in Florence, Wendell was the ideal companion. First, even though this was early on in the field-reports era, he and I had worked together enough so that we could share the duties of photo-journalism. We had about three hours to get whatever we were going to get; being with Wendell meant that we could go quickly to the site of the explosion, quickly determine that there wasn't much to get there except a picture of a hole in the ground. It meant that I could then leave him to take those pictures and get on film the story from the owner of the land, and I could go downtown and try to figure out how to make a story of the incident that justified all the charters and rushing and sleeplessness.

Because that was the problem as we learned how to do these things. Here was an important story, and if you were the editor of *The New York Times*, you used maybe a dozen paragraphs from your man on the scene, and another dozen from the man at the air base from which the errant plane had flown, and a long story from Washington on how this could happen and how often it could happen.

But the challenge to us was to get something from the scene that would illuminate the story for television without corrupting it for journalism. We could not do a background piece in depth—in those days of a fifteen-minute broadcast, two minutes was a long piece, and besides, if we started going into depth we would miss that evening's broadcast, and the flavor and importance, the atmosphere that would make an important story important to the people watching us, would be gone twenty-four hours later. (In all candor, what would also be in my mind was that if we missed that night's broadcast, our little cameo would probably not get on the next night.)

In this particular case I wandered up and down the main

street briefly and talked to some people. They were fascinated by their sudden notoriety, but in general disapproved of the Air Force for dropping a bomb on them. What occurred to me there was the Barber Shop Device; I invented it that day, and though so far as I remember I never used it in just that form again, I was identified with it, as Bob Allison became identified with doing civil-rights pieces from the top of the courthouse, leaning out a window over the statue of a Confederate soldier in the square below. And as Charles Kuralt became identified with doing his stand-uppers sitting down at a café table, beaming over a cup of coffee. (A "stand-upper" is the explanatory or introductory or closing part of a report, done by the reporter looking at the camera. The British call it a "piece to camera.") These were all ways we figured out to do the thing we wanted to do, and they're still being used. They sound simple now, like two-projector pieces, but we had to invent them before they were simple.

What I did was this: when Wendell Hoffman finished his shooting at the scene and came into town, we took the camera into a barber shop and aimed it up at two barbers and their customers and just let the four of them talk about the bomb incident. It was mildly forced conversation, but in the five or six minutes that we recorded there were some real, evocative comments that we probably would not have gotten in a straight interview. It worked, and it is what made the piece a little better than any other film report that night.

Then it was back to the charter, and to the connecting flight, and goodbye to Wendell, and me off with the film to Washington. Film to laboratory around three o'clock. Then developed film to me, waiting with Neil Strawser, who had other film stories to put together, at the editing rooms about 4:00 or 4:30. An hour, roughly, to edit and script the story before starting the long ride to the studios in northwest Washington. Compared to a lot of stories, a luxury of time.

So that is how it was, on a standard sort of fireman's story, in the late 1950's. Fifty dollars—less the twenty percent —earned; a feeling when the 7:15 p.m. feed of the broadcast was over that it had been a decent job; a quick drink with a Washington friend; and then a race to the airport to make a nine-o'clock plane to La Guardia. And the drive to Connecticut, tired now, but making it home for the night. No family dinner that night, and no swim. But at least the presence of a husband and father in the house and him there for the pre-school breakfast, and then to the train and New York. I loved it.

THE THING THAT I DIDN'T REALIZE but was grateful for later is that in being the first correspondent out of television news, and in working out of New York rather than Washington, I got a wide range of experience in working with film. We had to be producers: in a sense, most of the stories we worked with had to be invented. I don't mean falsified, I mean given meaning with script and picture. The meaning wasn't something you had in mind when you went to the story; it was the true gist of the reporting you did when you got there. But it was the invention of reality. How to explain what I mean?

Well, if you are the White House correspondent for CBS News, which I was later, you have to know as much as possible about what your President is doing, you have to be on speaking terms with the right staff people, you have to listen and watch and chase and work very hard and be very good at the working. But the *story* on air, basically, is something the President did or didn't do—illuminated and evaluated, certainly, but in essence *his* story. But suppose your assignment one August day is to go to Udall, Kansas, where a year or so before had occurred one of the most disastrous tornadoes in history. It is the dog days of the year for television news; what Hewitt wants is a solid feature that will justify the use of some of the dramatic film of the tornado and its aftermath and will also, responsibly, say something about people and weather and calamity. How do the people in Udall feel about things now? There again is the challenge of Florence: the quick and accurate summary of how they feel is not a picture story. The problem again is to find a way in which the picture will tell you something that the facts cannot. It is not a bastardized journalism: a good writer for print tells you things, with the same facts, that a hack rewriteman does not. It is just doing it better.

In Udall the bottom line was, unsurprisingly, that the townspeople would just as soon not have another tornado, but didn't intend to spend the rest of their otherwise pleasant lives worrying about it. Get them saying that on film and you have the standard story. Make the *film* say that and you have the thing that sends you back to the airplane happy. Wendell and I did that in Udall with a young woman, a housewife and mother, who was hanging clothes on the line in her backyard. It was afternoon, and on hot August afternoons in the Middle West in August the big thunderheads build up to the south and west even while the sun is still blazing on you. It is always tornado weather somewhere on the horizon.

The lady was one of those beautiful midwestern women, full of her quiet life, open and lovely. We did a brief interview with her, and when that was over she looked a little guiltily at the basket of wet wash—diapers, I think— and at the drying sun overhead, and the towering and ominous clouds on the horizon. "Do you ever," I asked idly, "do you ever look up at those clouds while you're working and remember the day of the tornado, and worry?"

"All the time," she said. "Worry about where the kids are, and Bob, and dumb things like will the diapers get dry before it rains."

"Would you mind showing us?" I asked, and spoke to Wendell. What we got was the picture that made the story: the handsome woman with a diaper shaken out in her hands, two clothespins in her mouth, looking back over her shoulder at the gathering forms of black and yellow on the horizon. It could be construed as a kind of staging, I suppose, but my conscience was clear. It was what she did; we just asked her to show us. It was the kind of picture television has to have —small, for a small screen, and crystal clear.

It could be felt that it was a trivial story. That was probably the summer when Ike sent the Marines into Lebanon, or a similar summer, and when John Kennedy was organizing his plans for 1960, and when Lyndon Johnson, back at work after his heart attack, was wondering how he could ever be President. I've covered those important stories, too, and I like them, but I must admit to an overweening fondness for the good pictures and the good people you would never know otherwise, and who are, in the long run, considerably more important than the movers and the shakers. I loved that stuff, and so did Wendell.

That time there was no race for airplanes, because the feature could wait to be properly edited and scripted in New York. So we drove back to Kansas City and I checked into a hotel and called the house doctor. I had felt feverish and miserable all day. The doctor came and listened to my lungs and palpated my belly and said I had flu and gave me some pills and said it would be all right to catch the early-morning flight for New York. But in the course of his palpating he said, "My, that's a large liver. Have you ever had any problems?" I hadn't, but I fell into melancholy. It was not many months since Senator Joseph McCarthy had died of cirrhosis, and I thought what a pity, what a way for me to go before my fortieth birthday, and as soon as I got back to New York I went for blood tests and they came out all right. But I have been worrying about my liver ever since. Tornadoes don't scare me much. Livers do.

IT WAS IN THOSE DAYS that I was temporarily one of the chief CBS authorities on the space program. It wasn't much of a program in those days. It was all under the control of one branch or another of the military, and almost everything about it was regarded as a military secret except what the three services—jealously engaged in separate programs—chose to put out in press releases. The Russians had put Sputnik up a few months before and there had been an almost hysterical reaction in the United States. Innocent junior-high-school students suddenly found themselves dragooned into Saturday classes in remedial physics; engineers suddenly had more job offers than they could have dreamed of. The gloomiest view was that Sputnik, beep-beeping away in orbit, had exposed us to the world as a second-class, over-the-hill power.

At this juncture our hopes for recovery rested on the United States Navy, the Martin Company, and a thing about the size of a grapefruit called Vanguard, which the Navy proposed to shoot into orbit from Cape Canaveral in early December, 1957. The Navy explained in press releases that Vanguard was so much smaller than Sputnik not because our rocket that was to launch it was so much less powerful than theirs, but because our technology was so much more advanced that we didn't need that big a thing in order to make a beep-beep from space.

Charles von Fremd, who died a few years later, was then the chief CBS News correspondent at Canaveral, and I was sent down to assist him as Vanguard's launch date neared. Neither of us could have functioned without the film cameraman who had become the expert on how to take pictures of rocket launches, Paul Rubenstein of Tampa. Not because he had perfected the technique for filming, at long range, a launching, but because in those days everything at Canaveral depended on connections and rumors, and Paul had the connections and had mastered the analysis of the rumors. As noted, the rocket business then was regarded as a military operation. Launch times and sometimes launch results were classified information, and no unauthorized civilians, certainly no press, were allowed within ten miles of the launching pads. What you did was hang around in the bar of the Starlite Motel, and maybe one of the waitresses was married to a Martin man, or one of the bartenders had a wife who worked for an Air Force colonel who had heard some gossip about the Navy. Paul knew all these people, and we finally determined that Vanguard would be launched on December 6, 1957, somewhere between 8:00 a.m. and noon.

We worked out an elaborate plan to ensure that, while Russia might have beaten the United States, no one was going to beat CBS News. Chuck von Fremd and Paul went to the nearest beach that had an unobstructed view of the launch—ten miles away, but unobstructed. I went to the cottage that Chuck and his wife had on the beach in front of the Starlite. Chuck was to get film and description for the *Evening News*; I was the man who was to get the word to New York of the launch, so that CBS Television and Radio could intrepidly defeat NBC and ABC by getting the bulletin on the air first, even if it meant interrupting a commercial in a morning soap opera. They had worked out an elaborate system in New York to do their part, and put an executive on an open telephone line to the phone in the von Fremd living room, where Virginia von Fremd sat with the receiver at her ear. Out on the porch above the beach was this fearless reporter, eyes glued and glazed to a pair of binoculars. When dripping sweat from my forehead didn't obscure the glass, I could just barely see Vanguard, miles away, at its pad.

My eyes hurt and it was hot and I was afraid I wouldn't

know a launch if I happened to be focused on it when it happened; I had never seen one. But the system worked. At about ten o'clock I saw an unmistakable flash of flame, and the pencil-thin white rocket began to move. "There she goes!" I shouted. "There she goes!" shouted Virginia into the phone. "There she goes!" shouted the executive in New York, hanging up the phone there and then and charging off to get the bulletin on the air.

We beat ABC and NBC, certainly. There was only one problem. A tenth of a second after I shouted, "There she goes!" I shouted, "Hold it!" Something had gone wrong. The lovely, slender rocket was not continuing upward; it leaned and then fell, with a great deal more flash and smoke. Vanguard had exploded on ignition. Maybe the technology was *too* advanced. Certainly ours was; by the time I shouted "Hold it!" there was no one on the phone in New York.

It was the first really elaborate attempt by CBS News to cover a Canaveral launching. We got better later.

There were two other, better memories of those early days when the military was playing *I've Got a Secret* and before Walter Cronkite discovered and copyrighted the space program. One came a few weeks later when I was riding, very late at night, with Wendell Hoffman, bound from Lincoln, Nebraska, to somewhere. We had been dimly aware that the Army, seeing (a) a chance to retrieve American prestige against Russia, and, more importantly, (b) a chance to further embarrass the Navy, had been feverishly working at Huntsville, Alabama, to throw together a satellite and something to launch it with. Wernher von Braun, the

German who had developed the guided rocket missiles for Germany that hit London in the late stages of World War II, was in charge. That night there was a radio bulletin, fifty-six days after Vanguard fell over; the Army had launched Explorer I from Canaveral, and Americans could listen to the beep it was sending back to earth—a sweeter, truer beep than Sputnik's.

And very shortly after that I was at Canaveral when the Air Force made a perfect first launch of its powerful new rocket, the Atlas. I took the film and drove ninety miles to Orlando and put the story on the air from there. The fumbling and the hysteria in America's space effort, I said, may be over. It was. So was the era of listening for launch rumors in the bar and filming from ten miles away, the era of Rubenstein and Reasoner. The era of Cronkite and interservice cooperation and press tents convenient to the launch pads had begun. Go, baby, go.

I remember so many things from those fireman days— mostly, I suppose, of interest only to other relatively old-timers. Suitable now for evenings in some strange city on a *60 Minutes* assignment, having a drink after dinner with Walter Dombrow and remembering all the funny things on stories we worked on. Or boring a young correspondent, trying to convince him that even with the pictures the writing is still important. Or arguing with executives that something went wrong somewhere, that the broadcasts now are too much Washington, too portentous and full of politicians, and that the crews and correspondents ought to be back in Florence, South Carolina. Maybe in a harsher world of energy crisis and ecology and inflation you can't do it that way any more, but I suspect you can. I suspect the energy crisis is not in Washington, it is out there somewhere, and someone with a reporter's feelings ought to go out and look for it. It is a crisis of American minds more than anything else, and all the Washington people have something to sell. We buy too readily. I have often said that if I ran CBS News, I would close the Washington bureau. I don't suppose I would, but it would be tempting: close Washington up, but watch it, and if something besides self-servers talking to each other happened down there—as it would most days—send a crew and correspondent down there to cover it. Not a correspondent who is a flattered habitué of Washington, but some tough, informed kid who would be as questioning about Senator Proxmire as he would be about a hurricane in Lake Charles, Louisiana. Since the trend is to do more and more in Washington, and maybe even to place the news head-quarters there, I am at best a voice crying in the wilderness and at worst a gaffer mumbling in my beer about the good old days. But I admit it: in the mumbling I sometimes think that, except for *60 Minutes* and *CBS Reports*, we did it better then. Better even with cranky Auricons and bad sound and no field producers than now with electronic cameras, with instant knowledge of how good your picture is, and lovely color and crisp definition—fantastic cameras, but aimed at Al Ullman running for re-election. Or at a supermarket aisle while a voice over the meaningless picture reports on the cost-of-living index. The cost of living is out there some-where, too, fellows. How about some reporters? How about some guys who go out and find things out and come back and tell you, instead of some people listening to other people tell them?

You see how I get.

But I do remember, including the great mistakes. And including the occasional terror. Making a piece in the tattered remnants of an airplane—DC-6, I think—which the federal investigators had patched together at the far edge of the field in Wilmington, North Carolina, patched together so they could establish just where the man from Westport was when he set off the bomb that broke the airplane and dropped it and all its unwitting doomed to the ground. A travesty of an airplane, dramatic in its revelation of how fragile these great silver birds are. Making the piece, and then racing to the other side of the field to catch a plane to Washington—the exact same kind of plane, same airline, same color scheme. A nervous flight.

That was the night, I think, when out of four possible major errors in getting the piece on the air, we made all four. It happened this way: our film in those days was shot in one of two ways—reversal, like a color slide, or negative, like a still picture you have to make a print of. The director chose a button which either projected the reversal film directly or, if it was negative, did a clever thing called reversing polarity, which made negative film give a positive image on the air. The other decision was to choose a button which reproduced the sound either magnetically or optically, depending on what film was involved. And, as we noted previously, you had to do all this twice, at 6:45 and at 7:15. My film that day was negative and magnetic. At 6:45 the director did not reverse the polarity, and we had unintelligible, ghostly pictures and perfect sound. At 7:15 he corrected the picture but hit the optical sound button, and we had lovely pictures and no sound. Neither of us got fired.

Remembering the long walks in a hundred strange cities, the evening walks to justify the steak and martinis and the short sleep before an early call. Remembering the scary charters in heavy weather to Montgomery, and all the nights with the crews, and feeling, sort of, toward the end of this period that it was a young man's game and that I was getting stale, and then a rejuvenation when I hit the right story, and not knowing what lay ahead: that eventually Don Hewitt would figure out how to do all this on a proper scale, and keep the excitement going, in a program he wanted to call *60 Minutes.*

3

Little Rock

I WENT TO ARKANSAS FIRST in August of 1944; I got off the train in Fort Smith after a long trip from Los Angeles. It was my first time in the South and I didn't like it. I was being transferred from a unit at UCLA which consisted of twenty-six men of certified high intelligence studying pre-medicine at the behest and through the beneficence of the United States Army, and I had decided that medicine was not for me.

There were two primary reasons for the decision. In our accelerated biology laboratory, I was the only soldier who could not keep his pithed frog alive. I don't know whether you have ever pithed a frog. What you do is you hold the little rascal by the neck and insert a small scalpel into its head and then push it on down the spinal cord. If you do it right, you have a frog that is still functioning in many ways but really doesn't care much; you can hook it up to electrodes and run kymograph recordings of its nervous pattern and do other interesting things without causing it any discomfort. One of our little band kept his frog technically alive for four days. I pithed three frogs and none of them lived for more than three minutes. Looking forward to the time when I would be expected to perform equally delicate procedures on human beings, it seemed to me the moral thing to do was to resign from the pre-medical program. Also I was spending my lunch hours and weekend evenings with a dusty blonde named Betty who kept asking me if I wasn't uncomfortable lounging around in uniform in the fleshpots of Los Angeles when my fellow soldiers were invading France and starting up the long chain of islands to Japan. I told her that General Somervell had sent us a telegram, posted on the bulletin board of the Phi Gamma Delta House where we lived, which urged us not to be jealous of the fellows who were having all the fun in Normandy because, in the balance of the total war effort, what we were doing was equally important. She was unimpressed, and, considering the matter of the frogs, the increasing difficulty of organic chemistry, and the possibility that a grand gesture might so impress Betty that I would have a hell of a final weekend in Westwood, I resigned.

I expected to go back to the infantry, but instead was assigned to the 3613th Ordnance Evacuation Company in Camp Chaffee, Arkansas. That was why I had ridden three days on dirty trains from Los Angeles, most of the time wondering in a bemused way what I had done and why; the weekend had not been all that good, and line-soldiering in Arkansas as compared to Saturday-night hitchhiking on

Wilshire Boulevard looked increasingly unattractive. I took my first look at Arkansas and the South prepared to dislike it.

You come into Arkansas for the first time in August and the first thing you notice is the heat. There is an enveloping heat there in the late summer, a kind of wet haze that encloses you all day and night and leaves you, ten seconds after a cold shower, with a coating of a kind of slime, like a slug. I think the heat explains a lot of the South's historical problems. I don't see how, before air-conditioning, they got *anything* done, and I can see how it made them mean as snakes, and slow. This, especially for enlisted men, was definitely before air-conditioning. I remember lurching through the hilly country around Chaffee that late summer, learning what Ordnance we were supposed to Evacuate and how. What is harder to remember is how I felt about the South as opposed to how I felt about the Army, because it certainly never occurred to me then that I would learn to love the South.

After we of the 3613th evacuated ourselves from Arkansas, I didn't go back until the fall of 1957. That first return was a one-day incident; I was not the principal reporter for CBS News in that first fall of turbulence; I was filling in. But that day began a lasting association with Little Rock and Arkansas, and by the next spring I was the principal reporter for Little Rock. I have never done any job better.

To most reporters there comes one story which you always believe was the best job you have ever done. You feel absolutely on top of it. You know everything about it, the surface swirling and the reasons for the swirling, the good guys and the bad guys, why it happened and what should have been done and ought to be done. It is a feeling of mastery and confidence without arrogance; a feeling of love for every element of the story and all the people in it, not because they are all lovable but because you know them so well. I felt that way about Little Rock after a while. After a while. In candor I have to say that in my first days there I just followed Claude Sitton of *The New York Times* around because he knew where things were. But after a while I had it straight, and it's a story that deserves retelling here in some detail, I think.

The events that made Little Rock so reluctantly well known around the world, and which came to symbolize the problems of the first phase of school desegration, began with the case of a cute, fat little black girl named Linda Carol Brown, who lived in Topeka, Kansas, and had to walk past a nice, clean, white grade school to get to her black grade school some distance away. Her father, assisted by the National Association for the Advancement of Colored People (they were colored people then, or Negroes), filed suit in federal court, contending that the extra steps for Miss Brown violated several sections of the Constitution, and that the time had come to review and reject the historic doctrine that facilities for different races could constitutionally be separate as long as they were equal.

In 1954 Chief Justice Earl Warren and the court agreed with the Browns. In *Brown* v. *Board of Education*, they ruled for Brown, striking down the fifty-eight-year-old Plessy vs. Ferguson "separate but equal" decision. In succeeding decisions they made it plain this applied to the little Browns wherever they were, and directed the nation's school boards to make the necessary changes with "all deliberate speed."

The decision seemed to find Little Rock well prepared. Arkansas may have had a relatively low literacy rate, but there were plenty of people there who could read the handwriting on the wall. One of them was Superintendent of Schools Virgil Blossom, who with the board of education was ready with a plan for phased desegregation, beginning with the city's two high schools. It was desegregation based on residential areas, and it was to begin only after the opening of the new Hall High School in Pulaski Heights, where Little Rock's establishment lived. The suspicion was that the board and Blossom believed this would avoid opposition from most of Little Rock's white movers and shakers, since it would not involve putting any blacks in Hall for some years. The concept of bussing had not been developed, so the burden of this major change would fall on the working-class blacks and whites who lived around Central High School on 14th Street. The phrase "limousine liberals" had not been invented either, but it describes the way those working-class whites felt, with some justice, about the shaved and groomed and uninvolved residents of the Heights.

The Central High parents felt violated and powerless. In fairness, the bankers and lawyers and Chamber of Commerce merchants in the Heights didn't like desegregation either, but they had an early sense that rebellion against federal law would mean economic disaster for Little Rock, and for them the new plants and the new commerce that kept the city growing and its residents in turn spending and building were, maybe sadly, more important than the traditions of the South. As someone said, the color of integration was not black or white but money green. Little Rock, of course, had never been sure that it was Southern. Below the city the hot hills stretched down to the Delta and a plantation culture not much different from Mississippi; to the north and west the hills got higher and the flavor was more Appalachian than Southern; while in the city itself there was—in spite of the heat and about a twenty-three-percent black population—a midwestern feeling, an energy and pragmatism and devotion to "progress."

IT SHOULDN'T HAVE HAPPENED in Little Rock any more than maybe Des Moines. But maybe it had to happen somewhere: the major, identifiable confrontation between old custom and new conscience, between entrenched habit and entrenched fear and emerging strength and timid expectation. It is interesting to recognize that once the confrontation happened in Little Rock, once the two-year struggle there was resolved, no confrontation anywhere else was quite as bad as it might have been if Little Rock's agony had not occurred and the issue won by the moderate bourgeoisie. Governor Wallace might not only have stood in the schoolhouse door, he might have kept it closed for a while; the half-dozen dead in Mississippi might have been hundreds; the unseemly and almost comic brawling in South Boston nearly twenty years later might have been more like the grim horror of Belfast. Little Rock set a pattern for the South, a one-sentence lesson for its Establishment that, after Little

Rock, no Establishment seriously tried to contest: the Southern Way of Life is beautiful and gracious and charming—but it is not really worth fighting for.

The reason the big test happened in Little Rock rather than in some more likely place is simple: a complex and curiously engaging man named Orval Faubus. Faubus had been elected governor in the fall of 1954, and was looking forward to being elected again and again and again. In most ways, for Arkansas, he was a good governor. He had been, for Arkansas, riskily liberal in racial areas: more black men and women held responsible positions in state government than ever before; they were a substantial influence within the Democratic Party. Governor Faubus himself had no strong feelings about desegregation. He had lived in Chicago in an integrated school situation himself and it hadn't bothered him. He had, about race relations, no more strongly felt principles than he had about any other issues. He was a Snopes, I suppose, a recognizable American type of devious achiever, transparently a hypocrite and confidence-man. But the out-of-town reporters who got to know him so well could never quite dislike him, because it was his charm to admit his hypocrisy. He was conscious of no sham because to Faubus the shammers were the men and women of principle who wanted to desegregate Central High School— where none of their children and none of their friends' children were enrolled.

One example of Governor Faubus' technique: there came a point where there were almost daily press conferences in his reception room, and on one occasion I irritated him with a reasonably tough question. He more or less exploded at me as the cameras rolled, not quite calling into question the legitimacy of my parentage, but fairly close to that. The conference ended and he came over and put his arm around my shoulders. "Sorry as hell to have to do that to you, Harry," he said, "but you know how it is." If I didn't, I learned in Little Rock.

To northern liberals and the liberal reporters Faubus looked and sounded the part of a villain. He had that kind of swarthy and smiling face that is still best described as oily, his voice was backwoods unctuous and patently insincere. He had played fast and loose with Dwight Eisenhower. He was despised by Little Rock's intellectual and business community (in the South these two groups tend to be more synonymous than in most Northern towns). He was an embarrassment to the responsible Democratic parties of his neighbor states. He himself despised his allies in the White Citizens Council and the other segregationist groups. But he proposed to remain governor of Arkansas and he perceived where the votes were. They were in two large groups: the people who quite seriously believed that to mix the races in schools and at lunch counters was abhorrent and dangerous, and the people who had no strong feelings about that but who believed federal control of any internal matter that important was abhorrent and dangerous. Together, these groups probably included eighty percent of Little Rock's people.

The two long years of the Little Rock story began in the fall of 1957. After a long series of state and local court actions, there seemed to be no further way to delay the initial desegregation step—admission of nine carefully selected black youngsters to Central High. But just before opening day Governor Faubus announced that he had evidence to indicate there would be major violence if the blacks went to Central. He called out the National Guard, which surrounded the school and turned the blacks away. A lot of other people surrounded the school, too, and they cheered.

But this was direct defiance of a federal court order, and the action distressed a lot of people who didn't care particularly about the nine youngsters. It distressed moderate Southern Democratic governors. It even distressed Dwight Eisenhower, vacationing at the naval station in Newport, Rhode Island. He was not particularly liberal on race relations, and he had already begun to regret that he had named Earl Warren to be chief justice. But his understanding of the American system was that when a court told you to do something, you did it, whether you liked it or not.

There were attempts at compromise. Governor Faubus flew to Newport and talked to the President and gave him the impression he would stop defying the court. And indeed at the end of the next week Governor Faubus withdrew the Guard.

That made things ready for September 23, probably Little Rock's single worst day. The nine blacks came back to school. A thousand whites surged around the school. Little Rock police couldn't handle them, and at noon the nine black students were taken away. This was the day that produced the most dramatic and depressing pictures. The next day President Eisenhower sent eleven hundred members of the 101st Airborne Division into Little Rock, and the day after that, school reopened with the black students present and with no substantial violence.

The handling of the Little Rock problem, incidentally, illustrates a couple of things about Dwight Eisenhower, who even as this is being written has been substantially rehabilitated in the view of current history. Little Rock showed Ike at what liberals considered to be his worst—he declined, as a matter of policy, to act as a leader or persuader on issues that sharply divided his countrymen. His contention was that people should make up their own minds about segregation and race relations, and then elect legislators who would express their consensus in law. But once there was a law— from Congress or from the Supreme Court's interpretation of the Constitution—the President meant to enforce it.

And in the matter of enforcing this particular court order General Eisenhower demonstrated one of his basic military principles: if you must finally resort to force, the most efficient and humane thing to do is to use *overwhelming* force. He discussed this, some years later, in terms of both Little Rock and Vietnam. Inadequate force is a temptation to bloody resistance, said Ike. Overwhelming force, if you have it, brings quick order. I thought a couple of Southern experiences made his theory look good.

The slick professionals of the 101st Airborne moved in effectively and dispassionately; they were neither nervous, as National Guardsmen had proved to be, nor emotionally involved. They ringed Central High and brought immediate order. There was only one minor casualty that first morning of the federal presence—when a young civilian, part of the crowd being kept away from Central High by the soldiers, in a mood of rather touching optimism tried to take a rifle away from a paratrooper. The trooper, standing at port arms, moved his rifle smartly to the left and back, hitting the civilian in the face on the return trip. The civilian went to the ground bleeding moderately from the cheek, and the soldier returned to port arms, his countenance impassive. It was the last of the morning's violence; no one was killed or seriously injured all year in the Central High affair.

In contrast, when President Kennedy and his attorney general, Robert Kennedy, dealt with the desegregation of the University of Mississippi, they attempted at first to exercise a moral leadership, which white Mississippians found unimpressive. Then they sent in a couple of hundred federal marshals—political appointees, relatively untrained, in widely varying physical condition. That kind of inadequate force could not put a lid on the town; two men were killed on the first night.

So THERE WAS SOME KIND OF EDUCATION at Central High that year. But the segregationists and Governor Faubus—who was preparing to run for a third term in the fall of 1958—were not yet convinced. The governor got a series of laws out of the legislature, one of which permitted communities to close their schools, and to make alternative arrangements for private education. The question was put to the citizens of Little Rock on September 27, a Saturday, and put in words which purists might have considered emotionally toned. To vote to keep the schools open and to follow the court-ordered desegregation plan, you had to vote for "immediate integration of all schools." Nineteen thousand Little Rock citizens voted against that, 7,500 voted to keep the schools open even though they had to mark a ballot "for immediate integration," in which probably not 500 white voters believed.

So that was the second year. In 1958–59 there were no public high schools operating in Little Rock. The old school board, feeling with some justice that it had been on the firing line long enough, resigned en masse, and finally the Little Rock establishment decided it was time to get involved. They put up a slate of moderate businessmen in the special election for a new board, and three of them were elected, along with three strong segregationists.

The establishment—the bankers, the officers of the Chamber of Commerce, the people of the big utility company and the other major businesses—was concerned because the highly negative image that Little Rock had gained around the world was beginning to hurt. By the end of 1958 there were documented instances of businesses which had planned to locate or expand in Little Rock changing their mind. It was not a place where employees from other areas wanted to move. Orval Faubus and the White Citizens Council and the troops on the sidewalk in front of Central High School made money that was in Little Rock and the money that might have moved in nervous. The establishment was not responding to a strong moral feeling; it was reacting pragmatically to a situation that was clearly bad for business. In fairness to their moral position, many of them were also strongly upset at the damage done to a pretty good school system, and deeply worried about the injustice to a whole generation of their children—white and black. But they were not, for the most part, liberals; most of them would have denied even being moderates. They would have said they were realists. And, on a personal level, they were awfully tired of Orval Faubus.

The movers and shakers had waited too long to move and shake, however. They seemed stymied. They had a half a school board, but the other half was adamant. And they still had a city which seemed willing to do without public education rather than to have public education on federal terms. They needed some kind of issue to dramatize how bad things were, to give the essentially kindly good citizens of Little Rock an excuse to change their minds, to move out of the penumbra of Orval Faubus and the extremists.

In an incredible move, the extremists gave the moderates their issue. It happened on May 6, 1959, after a day of wrangling by the school board. Tired of three-three votes on the subject of teacher contracts for the following year, the three moderates on the board walked out, leaving the segregationists without a quorum. But the three segregationists ruled that they did have a quorum, and they fired forty-four teachers.

The establishment had its issue. The segregationist members were suddenly not knights defending the Southern Way of Life, but distasteful fellows who had fired forty-four well-known and, in many cases, well-loved teachers. It was a gargantuan error. Citizens who had been unimpressed by the risks Little Rock was taking in defying the federal government were suddenly outraged at the implication that old Miss Millie and the other teachers they had studied under were communist dupes and nigger-lovers. The alliance of liberals and moderates and "realists" moved fast and organized a recall election to get rid of the three segregationist board members. The segregationists, in some disarray, put together a countermove to recall the three moderates. The people of Little Rock, voting for forty-four people some of them had known all their lives, recalled the segregationists and kept the moderates.

There is a note I would like to interject here, stolen from E. B. White (you could be a pretty good writer, stealing things from E. B. White). In the preface to his *Subtreasury of American Humor* White pointed out that Clarence Day had written a lot of wonderful verse and other material about man- and woman-kind, and that no one ever paid much attention. Then he wrote *Life with Father* and made himself safe for posterity. White's conclusion and advice to writers: "Don't write about Man, write about *a* man." Something like that happened in Little Rock.

Anyway, from then on it sounds simple. The county board of education named three people the moderates could live with to the board. The board moved to reopen the high schools in August. They did reopen, without substantial violence, and with a token black population—even in Hall High. The Little Rock story, as an international symbol of American division, was over—and no desegregation story to come after it would have quite the drama or the importance, although a lot of them had more blood.

THE THING ABOUT LITTLE ROCK is that it was where television reporting came to influence, if not to maturity. As in the case of the Vietnam war a decade later, things might have been very different if it weren't for the new impact of television news: you could not hide from it. In the 1850's a British detachment might fight a desperate battle at the Khyber Pass and a week later the London papers would have an account; it probably takes that kind of delay and the filtering of the blood and smell through a writing reporter to make imperialism possible. Even World War I, where the still camera came of age, went largely unseen until Laurence Stallings published *The First World War*, a book of photographs, in the 1930's. *Life* magazine covered World War II in great and sometimes grisly detail, but it took television to show you the war in Vietnam relentlessly every night to force a democracy to finally make a democratic decision about a war—a democratic decision in which the citizens themselves made up their minds on something very like first-hand evidence.

It was like that in Little Rock, and by and large the young men of television did a better job than the people of the printed word—with, of course, notable exceptions on both sides.

The key was understanding the story, and in turn there are two keys to understanding most stories. One is that there are always at least two sides to any story. The other is that the world doesn't have many real villains, very many real bad guys, if you define a villain as a person who *thinks* of himself as a villain. I've only been aware of two figures in the news during my career with whom I would not have shaken hands if called to deal with them professionally. I suppose that what Thomas Jefferson called a decent respect for the opinion of mankind requires me to identify those two. They were Senator Joseph McCarthy and a man named Paul Krassner or something like that who published a magazine called *The Realist* in the 1960's. I guess everyone knows who McCarthy was. Krassner and his *Realist* were part of a '60's fad—publications attacking the values of the establishment—which produced some very good papers and some very bad ones. Krassner not only attacked establishment values; he attacked decency in general, notably with an alleged "lost chapter" from William Manchester's book, *The Death of a President*. To paraphrase critic Clive Barnes' remarks about a movie: *The Realist* was the kind of paper that gives dirty papers a bad name. My grounds for despising them were that, based on their speech and actions, they had to *know* they were villains, but I suspect that even those two, who seemed execrable to me, thought of themselves in a much better light. And in Little Rock the people leading the opposition to desegregation, with the exception of Governor Faubus and a few other opportunists, did not see themselves as oppressors of black human beings, but as defenders of a system that worked best for both whites and blacks. There isn't anything startling about this conclusion, but it seems to me to have a major relevance to how a reporter does his job. Accepting the fact that most people don't think of themselves as wrong or evil, you can then report their behavior with a kind of recognition of dignity which is always deserved at the outset of coverage, a kind of professional detachment akin to the "willing suspension of disbelief" with which a civilized person approaches a new play or novel. Then let the *reporting* descry the evil, if it is there. You are not on hand merely to fill in the blanks of your own preconceptions.

This does not in any way mean soft reporting. It means being fair.

So we always tried to remember that there were 100,000 people in Little Rock, and that on the worst day not more than a thousand or so of them were behaving badly in front of Central High—and a lot of those were from out of town, holidayers from Mississippi. We tried to remember that Daisy Bates, the leader of the black effort, and Jimmy Karam, of the White Citizens Council, both quite sincerely believed that they were right.

And, as a corollary, since you never start out by assuming there is a clear line between the bad guys and the good guys, you have to remember that the heroes are not all heroic either. In Little Rock that meant remembering that the establishment which moved so late to straighten things out was composed of people for the most part acting out of understood, self-perceived self-interest, not out of morality.

It was a great story to test all of these unformed feelings I had about what reporting ought to do . . . and the best evidence I had was that I came out of Little Rock with so many friends on all sides of the story. Even Orval Faubus— and that's detachment.

It is perhaps fortuitous that on the night I am trying to make sure I've said all I should about Little Rock there is on CBS a fictionalized account called *Crisis at Central High*, based on a story by a teacher who went through all that. I watched the first hour and found nothing offensive to my sense of how things had gone. Of course, the program did not deal with journalism's role. I, for obvious reasons, am most concerned with journalism's role, and what this story taught us, the guys who worked with the cameras, the men and women—not many women then, naturally—who came to love or hate Little Rock, and who, I think, did a pretty good job, overall, of showing the rest of the country what was happening there.

I remember a seemingly irrelevant thing. In 1951, when I was much younger and not much smarter than I am now, I made a decision to take a young family to Manila. My sister, my only immediate relative, was distressed, and she talked to my Aunt Maurine. If you come from Iowa, you talk to your Aunt Maurine. If anything has really gone wrong with America in my lifetime, it is that there aren't enough Aunt Maurines any more, and that not enough nephews and nieces talk to their Uncle Harold. I don't think this is a defect in the nephews and nieces. I think it is an inappropriate reticence in their Uncle Harold.

Anyhow, my sister talked to Aunt Maurine about my taking three children and a wife to Manila in what, she correctly figured, was a spirit of frustration and adventure. And Aunt Maurine, who had with Uncle Harold done some things in her youth in a spirit of frustration and adventure, said, "Poor boy, doesn't he know everywhere is just the same?"

I'd argue some of that. Manila was not just the same—but in a way it was. But learning that Manila was comfortable and interesting for a boy from Iowa prepared me for Little Rock and for being a good reporter there. Little Rock was one of the great crises of the American spirit in my lifetime, and it sort of came out all right. (Never mind for the moment that now Little Rock has most of the problems of all American cities, racial included.)

I guess what I should do is tell you how I gathered material for this chapter, which I haven't used much of. My great friend out of Little Rock is a man called Everett Tucker. He was the fellow chosen by the establishment to be point man for the reopening of the schools. He was the president of the new school board which brought the schools back without either state interference or federal supervision after the election that turned on the voters' feeling about the forty-four teachers. Tuck, I think, to this day would resent being called a liberal. Certainly I had many letters from white liberals who felt my own close association with Tucker showed I was rejecting my presumed liberality. Oddly enough—and I obviously don't mean "oddly"—I didn't get any letters like that from the blacks I knew.

What Mr. Tucker and his friends in the white establishment wanted was to get the schools open, to sap the influence of Orval Faubus, and to resume the industrial boom in Little Rock. He did it. I remembered so many good talks with him that I decided to ask him to get together some of the other establishment people for a lunch in Little Rock in the summer of 1978 and talk about what had happened and why, while I let a tape recorder run. I have to say that, using the tape recording and some printed stuff from the *Arkansas Gazette* of those days, I have checked some dates from that era, but not much else. What that lunch did for me was what tonight's television program did: remind me how many of the people, white and black, southern and northern press, remember how it was, and how strongly some of them felt one way or another. It especially reminded me of how the *good* television people felt strongly they wanted to get it right.

The consensus of that 1978 lunch was that Orval Faubus had been the villain. But is it not possibly true that you cannot have a great American morality play without a villain? Little Rock was a great American morality play— the first one that television covered. We did fine.

A requisite of a story called *Before the Colors Fade* is that you have to remember some of the humanness of the people involved. I was a person involved, and I feel inclined to add an example of my humanness. Roughly fifteen years after Central High reopened, an echo of Little Rock made me feel, for the first time, older, if not old.

The story involves an assistant to Orval Faubus, one of those big, rangy jobs that come down out of the hills and brighten up the streets of so many Arkansas towns. We all flirted with her; on the basis of no substantive evidence, we all felt—particularly me—that she looked with particular favor on one of us. In one of those portentous Augusts I saw a lot of her in the office, and suddenly there was the Arkansas State Fair, and a cocktail party attendant thereon in the Sam Peck Hotel (in those days, one of the world's great hotels). Oriana or Elfabel or whatever the hell her name was was to be there, and there was a sort of understanding that we would go out to dinner afterward. We were sitting cozily on a couch munching Vienna sausages and drinking indescribably horrible bourbon when the man who was to be the star of the State Fair's nightly stage show came in—a great country singer named Rex Allen. He was four feet taller than me, gracious, witty, intelligent, and wearing a white suit with sequins, a cowboy hat, and boots. Have you ever seen a small child look at a chocolate ice-cream cone with sprinkles? That was Oriana or Elfabel or whatever. I relaxed, and I have never tried to make time with an assistant since.

What about feeling old, you say? Well, fifteen or so years later I was driven every day to work in New York, and I listened to a country-music station. (I like country music, and Fred Friendly wouldn't approve of that either.) One day I heard the first real hit record by Rex Allen, Junior. When you hear a hit record by a man whose father stole your girl, it's time to quit. Right? No.

4

Saturday and Sunday News

I N THE LATE SUMMER and early fall of 1960 I felt pretty
gloomy, professionally. Things were going very well
indeed for the profession (craft, I think we decided earlier)
but not very well for me at all. The second correspondent to
be named out of television at CBS News, Charles Kuralt, had
broken past me on the rail and was many lengths ahead. He
was working with the newly developed Eyewitness technique
and had been given custody of a prime-time program, Friday
nights, called, indeed, *Eyewitness to History*. The idea came
out of the rapid familiarity with the use of video tape which
developed, fortuitously, out of Dwight Eisenhower's fondness
for getting out of the White House and traveling somewhere
and being cheered in the streets. Tape made it possible for
someone like David Schoenbrun to stand in the streets of
Paris and describe the tumult and the shouting as if he were
at that moment on the air—present tense and all that. Then

the tape could be put on one of the new commercial jets and patched together with other reports in New York and put on the air that night. *Eyewitness to History*, as a program, was the result of somebody's bright idea that if we could do that on demand for a presidential trip, why couldn't we do it on a weekly basis, picking the major news story of that week and throwing all of CBS News' resources into it for a polished Friday-night program? It was a good idea—not at all like the later local news programs of the seventies that were called *Eyewitness News*. There was no joking around in the studio and no long and scalloped hair. It was a good program; the only major fault in it from my standpoint was that it was not mine.

In the fall of 1960 I was asked to do a field report for *Eyewitness to History*, to make something of the World Series between the New York Yankees and the Pittsburgh Pirates for the broadcast anchored by my friend Kuralt. Working for Kuralt, close friend, twelve years my junior chronologically and six weeks my junior as correspondent, was a blow to my pride, and my reaction to it made me ashamed. I sulked and behaved badly. Earlier that year the program director of WCBS-TV in New York had asked my superiors not to assign me as a substitute on any local news programs. Being banned this way was a blow to my pocket-book and made me poor.

In those days substituting was the way relatively junior correspondents, particularly those whose main work was in television, made their money. The local newscasts were staffed by CBS News correspondents—Douglas Edwards, Ron Cochran, Ned Calmer—and when they were sick or on vacation or assignment, the rest of us got a chance. I think the fee was $25 for the five-minute segments of the early evening news, maybe twice that for the longer eleven-o'clock. The money was a great help, and working in a studio was fun, too—makeup and stage managers and lights and cameras.

I had not substituted for anyone very often, and I suppose I was pretty bad. But I felt hurt as well as wounded financially, and I asked the assignment editor why WCBS didn't want me. He explained that the program director at the station felt that, while I was a reasonably good field reporter, I would never make it in studio work—that I had no presence, and that I did not open my mouth when I talked, probably the result of an adolescent reticence about showing bad teeth. I don't know where that program director is now.

It isn't even that the director was wrong. Years later, co-anchoring the evening news for ABC with Howard K. Smith, I got a letter from a deaf person. Howard and I, she said, were virtually useless to her as broadcasters because we didn't open our mouths and articulate the words in a way to help her lip-reading. "Howard is terrible," she wrote, "and as for you, Mr. Reasoner," she went on, "if you ever fail in the news business, you should do very well as a ventriloquist."

By 1973 that was all right, I could show the letter as a joke. But in the fall and winter of 1960 and the beginning of 1961 I felt pretty bad. It was quite clear that I could go on being a CBS News correspondent all my life and get the comfortable pension when I retired, but that I was tabbed as a journeyman, as one of the men who didn't quite make it. And the trouble was I had risen so fast, and acquired enough of a reputation, that none of the fun jobs the journeymen had was going to be offered to me. No one was going to assign me to Rome or London; I was needed in New York. But I was a little senior to chase stories out of New York, and, besides, by then the bureau system was beginning to develop, and the new civil-rights stories in the South were being covered by men and crews out of Atlanta. I had had a good summer in 1960. I had gone to Manila in advance of President Eisenhower's trip to the Far East and met a young woman who became one of the six great woman friends of my life (that "six" is the correct number as of 1981, but chances are it will hold up); I had taken the family by car to Los Angeles for my first political convention—as a reporter, that is—and had performed creditably, and then Charlie Kuralt and I had driven together to Chicago for the Republican convention that nominated Richard Nixon. But then it was fall and Pamela was in Manila and Charles Kuralt was running *Eyewitness* and— since I was too important to leave New York and there wasn't anything happening in New York, I was asked to do some radio news.

I didn't know at the time that, whether fortuitous or not, it could have been a part of some master plan for my development. I thought it was a putdown. I was a child and a molder of television news, and radio scared me a little. I didn't realize that the necessity of working and reading out two ten-minute radio broadcasts a day was going to be very good for both my writing and my voice. I knew the money was nice—it was sometimes up to an extra $1,000 a week. But to me—watching Kuralt on Friday nights, watching Edwards on the *Evening News*, lusting for the company of film crews and the scared arrival at a story, not knowing if you could handle it but also knowing, cold, that you could—it was a backwater. The more veteran editors and correspondents were up on the radio floor at 485 Madison: so was Murrow, of course, but I was so dumb I thought the place was fusty.

But I found myself liking it, and learning things from the people there, and beginning to fool around a little with the scripts. The thing is, the first obligation of an hourly radio newscast, at least at CBS, was to assume that for some unknown percentage of your audience that was the only news they would hear that day. So in the ten minutes minus commercials (six minutes now, as, even at CBS, pressure from radio affiliates has steadily eroded news time) you wanted to make sure that you touched every major story of the day. And every newscast included at least one report from the field. So, ostensibly, there wasn't much time to fool around. But you can pack a lot of stories into two or three minutes, and along with the percentage of people who had heard no other news, you knew there were a lot of folks who had heard the same news a half-dozen times since they woke up that morning. So you found ways to keep from being bored yourself, without clowning, and in the process you hoped to keep some of the people out there in their cars and kitchens from being bored. There was a ten-day story, I remember, about the hijacking of a Portuguese ocean liner; I finally began writing that one like a soap opera; it worked.

Ernest Hemingway died and I wrote his obituary in Hemingway style; it wasn't all that good, but it wasn't bad. And you read the news wires carefully because sometimes the way you can make a story a little different is a nugget down in paragraph forty-two. My favorite was the announcement of some major Washington appointment. Down in paragraph forty-two was a statement from the man's secretary. He certainly deserves the job, she said, he works so hard— why, since he arrived in Washington he has made ninety-five flights across the Atlantic. I figured that left him in Europe, and said so.

So, except for a couple of major television stories that did happen in New York, and except for my executive flirtation (see Chapter 6), that fall and winter passed quietly. We lived then in an old converted barn; it was just a barn which for forty years or so had functioned as a summer house and had had some heating pipes tacked to its ceiling. No window on the two floors was the same size as any other; the upstairs floor was linoleum and the bedrooms crazy shapes separated by wallboard, but the children liked it. I would sit in the driveway on my days off and watch the little kids, and we would swim in the millpond, and for the first time in my life I was making more money than I was spending, and we knew some nice people and we were beginning to love Connecticut. But there was still the nagging feeling that I had been passed over, like a career Navy officer, and that I was going to be a lieutenant commander forever. I wanted the gold braid.

That is how things stood on a Saturday morning in April 1961. The telephone rang around eight o'clock. I and one child—Ellen, I suppose—were the only people awake and downstairs. Jack Cowden was on the phone. He was a lifelong worker at CBS, a vice president for promotion and public relations, a close friend who lived in Westport. He asked me if I had seen *The New York Times* that morning. I said no; in those days we didn't have a paper delivered, I brought them home from work. "You might go out and spend a dime on a copy," Jack said, "I estimate today's edition is worth about a million dollars to you."

What was in the *Times* that morning was a column by Jack Gould, then and for another eight or nine years the unquestioned doyen and arbiter of television criticism. And what Jack Gould—incidentally, I never did meet him—had chosen to do to fill a Saturday column was to talk about CBS Television's *Eyewitness to History* and about my radio news broadcasts. What he said was:

> As for Reasoner, of course, he is anything but an unfamiliar figure on TV. But for the moment he is appearing more frequently and regularly in the expanded hourly news coverage on the radio side of C.B.S.
>
> Mr. Reasoner's chief contribution is to take the curse off the lifeless wire service prose of hourly newscasts. To items that already may have been broadcast several times he imparts a turn of the phrase that catches a listener's attention and he is not hesitant in using a touch of his own dry humor where circumstances warrant.
>
> If the individuality of Mr. Reasoner's broadcasts

73

reflects a broader C.B.S. policy to encourage members of its news staff to be themselves and not echo a corporate pear-shaped tone, the network could discover that its news problems were not as formidable as it may have thought.

The following then happened in what seemed like rapid succession: Frank Shakespeare, the general manager at Channel 2, WCBS-TV, the flagship station from which I had been banned, asked if I would be interested in permanent assignment to their Saturday-night early and late news. And my superiors in the news division asked if I would like to do the three-minute news insert on a new morning program they were planning for the fall. That was a program called *Calendar* and, as it turned out, I not only did the news but was co-host on it for two years; but that's another chapter, including another of the six women friends.

I began the Saturday-night local news segment quite soon after that: a five-minute chunk at seven o'clock, with two other men—sometimes one man and the late Carol Reed with the weather—filling out the then accepted routine of five minutes of weather and five minutes of world news. And then my own ten minutes at eleven o'clock.

I was ready, but if it hadn't been for the months of radio, I would not have been ready. I would have been as stiff and somber as in the few tries that had led to being banned. Now I was loose; I was not afraid to horse around some; I knew how to write it and how to read it. That was the fall when a program called *Gunsmoke* became an hour instead of a half-hour, and *Gunsmoke*, the most popular program on television, led in to our eleven-o'clock news. It was the year when Channel 2's *Late Show*—fairly recent movies in the years before the networks carried movies—was at its peak of popularity, and the *Late Show* followed our news. It was a piece of cake. That October, Channel 2 took a full-page ad to brag about its achievements—first in New York in entertainment and news, first in sports, first in lovability and civic consciousness. And in the long list of firsts, one which said: "In October, *The Saturday Night Late News* with Harry Reasoner was the most popular program in the nation." Not the most popular *news* program, but, market by market and in the biggest market, the most heavily watched program of any kind. *Gunsmoke* and the *Late Show* and the people who stayed over for the news and tuned in early for the news were the main reasons, but what we were doing with the broadcast didn't hurt. We were doing several things.

And when, in the seventies, I have been tempted to unreasonable criticism of various local news programs, I think back to some of the things we did and temper my judgment. On a Saturday when there had been a major horse race and a heavyweight fight and maybe a World Series game, we noted, for instance, that the programs that night were full of interviews with the winners. On our budget it was impractical to get the horse or the fighter or the winning pitcher, and, besides, the stagehands in that studio had never had to deal with a horse. But Irv Drasnin and I noted that it was also the day when the annual Charlotte-to-New-York homing-pigeon race had ended. The winner, an attractive doe (doe is probably not what you call female pigeons), was right there in Manhattan. We brought her to the studio and interviewed her.

I don't mean to imply that it was *Saturday Night Live*. On the night that the East Germans were discovered to be constructing a wall between their territory and West Berlin, we didn't interview any pigeons. But we established a principle which was somewhat new to CBS: when there is no overriding, grabbing news, the way out is not to be dull. It is either to pick that night to use some solid piece of background or investigation—which somehow didn't seem *right* at eleven o'clock on Saturday night—or play a little with the news. We probably could not have done that if Mr. Paley had been a regular watcher or if it had been a network program. But the general manager of WCBS loved the program and gave us almost complete latitude. And I think the kind of thing we did on Saturday night locally made it easier for me when I moved to the Sunday-night network show.

I also established another thing on Saturday nights—the habit of writing, as I had on radio, something a little different for the end of the broadcast. On both Saturdays and Sundays we were careful never to make it a rule, but we looked for things that would be suitable. Sometimes a piece of film that didn't fit anywhere else, sometimes something that seemed funny, sometimes a little extra piece on an item of news that struck us as poignant or ridiculous.

In possible anticipation of a discussion with Richard Salant, the president of CBS News, a discussion which really never came about, I structured in my mind a defense of flippancy and other diversions; news broadcasters should not be humorists, I agreed in advance to a charge that never came, but if the news itself, viewed in a certain way, reveals wit or insight or comment, it's all right to go ahead. So we did.

We called these things end-pieces, and I quote two of them here—one from the Saturday-night local, and one from a year or so later on the Sunday news:

> Ernie Kovacs died in a car accident in Hollywood this morning, and the guess has to be it was the most widely discussed news event of the day—one man's death in a world where everybody dies. This always happens when a man who belongs to the public, a man whom everyone knows, comes to a sudden end. The sense of loss and tragedy is heavy and immediate.
>
> An event like this hits us wherever we are on a Saturday morning—in a supermarket, on a skating rink, self-satisfied in a late bed—with the old promissory note of our own mortality in a way that generalized warnings from the National Safety Council never could.
>
> All prayer books ask for protection from sudden death. It is nice to think we will have a warning, time to think things out and go in bed, in honor and in love. Somebody dies in an unprepared hurry and you are touched with a dozen quick and recent memories: the sweetness of last evening, the uselessness of a mean word or an undone promise. It could be you, with all those untidy memories of recent days never to be straightened out.

There's a shiver in the sunlight, touching the warmth of life that you've been reminded you hold only for a moment.

Captain Charles White, the Eastern Airlines pilot who died in the crash of his Constellation yesterday, will likely be remembered as one of the great heroes of his profession. Most men in skilled work train themselves all their lives for one peak moment when everything they know and all their heart is called for, and they never have that moment or they botch it just a little. The moment came to Captain White— the moment he practiced for in combat missions over Germany and twelve thousand hours altogether flying big airplanes—and he apparently did everything just right. As a result, some fifty people are alive who might logically have expected to be dead.

After the collision, his plane was unflyable. But he flew it—giving some sense to its crazy motion by alternately powering engines on one side and then another, warning his passengers, and then picking out a field and coming in as softly as you can with that many tons at that kind of speed with no control —coming in flat and uphill—so that before the airplane burned up, almost everyone got out alive.

And now, tonight, Eastern Airlines tells us something else about Captain White: his body was found in the passenger cabin. Eastern's conclusion is that he could have gotten out, but that he died because he went back to see to the safe evacuation of his passengers.

The pride in a man like this radiates out in lessening circles of intimacy—from his family to his fellow employees at Eastern, to all pilots, to all his countrymen, and finally the pride you have in just being a member of the same species.

That's the news. This is Harry Reasoner. Goodnight.

Those were both serious, which wasn't typical, and they were both fairly long, which they didn't have to be. But they were liked; there is nothing more pleasant in this craft than meeting someone who remembers something you wrote five years ago. And, as noted, they don't have to be long. One of my favorites, and the favorite of Joyce Wilson of Dallas, Texas, was fifty words or so long on the Sunday night of one of Elizabeth Taylor's weddings. It went something like this:

Elizabeth Taylor, the American actress, and Richard Burton, the Welsh actor, were married today in Montreal. They met two years ago while working on the movie *Cleopatra* in Rome and have been good friends ever since.

That's the news. This is Harry Reasoner, CBS News. Goodnight.

5

Murrow

I T IS A STRANGE WAY to begin a chapter about Edward R. Murrow to say that probably he never did all he could for television news, but there is a way of thinking about it that makes that true. And it does not affect something else that is true: if it had not been for Edward R. Murrow and his close friendship with William Paley, television news might have developed very differently. We might have very dull and nominal news, as the British do. Or very sexy and trivial and irresponsible network news, as some American local stations do, or the sort of thing the British have in print journalism. American commercial journalism, in ink or pictures, is, when it's good, very much a matter of tradition. You get a tradition established, and you have made it difficult for small people to corrupt it, even when it would seem to be to someone's commercial advantage in an enterprise that is extremely commercial.

The way Edward R. Murrow helped was possible also because of World War II. In the reporting of that war he stood alone in the national mind. He and the men he recruited from 1939 on were the daily historians of that war on radio. I assume the NBC networks were covering the war, too, but I suggest that out of any literate group of Americans now over fifty-five, the average man could name two or three of the CBS News war reporters—names like Murrow, Smith, Collingwood, LeSueur, Hottelet. I'd bet the same average man couldn't name more than one other broadcast reporter, probably Raymond Gram Swing.

So, as the war ended, and as television began to look as if it would eventually dominate the broadcast scene, Murrow was a hero within and without his profession. And he was the close friend of Mr. Paley (I *know* I say "Murrow" and then "*Mr.* Paley." I doubt that I will ever be senior enough to leave off the "Mr." even in my thoughts), the chairman of CBS. This meant that three things happened. First, it was established at CBS and by osmosis at the other networks that network news would be responsible, serious sometimes to the point of pompousness and portentousness, and absolutely independent of the influence of the advertisers whose purchases supported it. Second, that network news would be free-spending, in spite of the fact that at that time no one foresaw that news could ever turn a profit. It would not hesitate to spend money for good reporting and for a kind of look of class. And, third, it was established that the correspondent, the face the people saw and the voice they heard, would be not only the central figure to the audience but a figure of substantial influence in what he was asked to do and how he would do it. If it had not been for the happy synergism of World War II, William Paley, and Ed Murrow, Walter Cronkite might have been impossible as a fact of television; might today have been president of United Press International. (And what a waste, even if it might have made my life simpler.)

Then how did this great man fail to do all he could for television news? Basically, it was because he never really liked doing it. With Fred Friendly he did great things in *See It Now* and *CBS Reports*, but he never had the fondness for the day-to-day detritus and headaches of television that would have led him to be CBS News' first daily television newscaster, which he certainly could have been. I don't know why; I did not know him well, but I suspect that it was not a contempt for television but a feeling that what *he*—Murrow —could do he could do better on radio; he wanted to help and to do good things in and for television, but he didn't love it. So he went on doing his nightly radio news program, and working with Friendly some, and brooding about the nature of American journalism. But at a time when his influence was incredible, he did not, on his own, do innovative things in television. He did a program called *Person to Person*, which was technically innovative but an embarrassment of triviality.

He came into my life on three occasions, two of them significant to my career. I obviously am not and never was one of "Murrow's Boys," the staff he put together to cover World War II for broadcasting. At the same time, I might not be where I am if it had not been for Murrow. None of us might be here if it weren't for him, of course.

Occasion One: I had been introduced to Murrow after I joined CBS. It was, for me, something like a private audience with the Pope for a believing parish priest. And then a situation began to develop at CBS of which I was only dimly aware. What it was, I guess—and I am not the expert on this—was an estrangement, a clash of personalities, between Murrow and CBS President Frank Stanton—an equal giant of this craft in his way, but not, apparently, personally compatible with Murrow. Murrow said some strong things about the corruption of television news by commerce, and Stanton resented them, and the newspapers loved all this internecine conflict among giants, and it was finally announced that Murrow would take a sabbatical, a year off, and think, and smoke, I suppose.

It occurred to Don Hewitt, the producer of the evening news, and even to some of our brighter executives, that since this was a front-page story in every major paper, perhaps Douglas Edwards should report the story and we should seek an interview with Murrow. I was around, I was the hot-shot reporter, and when Murrow agreed to meet a reporter at the Overseas Press Club and submit to questioning in front of a camera, I was told to go down and do it.

What I didn't know—I had not been around CBS long enough to know—was the sensitiveness of the whole thing: the feeling among many of the people I worked with and for that Murrow despised their little electronic operation, that he felt the integrity and reputation of CBS News reposed uptown in the old radio area and that we were a rather unsavory offshoot. I didn't know and nobody told me. In retrospect, I could see that I was sent off in somewhat the spirit of a World War I suicide mission, but I was a little slow. Edward R. Murrow, charging CBS and specifically Dr. Stanton with presiding over a kind of commercially influenced lapse from greatness, was going to be off the air for a year; it was a major news story. I knew the questions I would like to ask, and I went to the interview site with no realization that I was, in a way, in the middle of not so much a power struggle as a family feud.

I did one thing, out of my awe, that I had never done for another subject: I offered to outline my general line of questioning in advance. Murrow said he thought that would be inappropriate. Even then, torn though he must have been, taking his late afternoon for this scritchy chore, he could no more help giving a lesson or reminding a youngster of the principles of his craft than he could be discourteous or unkind.

We did the interview. I asked him about the substance of his charges against television—that its programming was increasingly tawdry, that there seemed to be no room for thorough news programming, that it was, in effect, becoming a carnival. Then I asked him what he had done, with his prestige and influence, to change this. I asked him how he could criticize general entertainment programming and yet make a fortune from *Person to Person* while declining to do anything for the struggling and embryonic area of day-to-day television news. He seemed mildly surprised at the questions, but he didn't duck them, and we took the film back to the laboratory and Hewitt made a good two-minute cut from it and it was broadcast that night.

By the time I got home that night there was the first of

the telephone messages. There were several more calls that night and four or five notes to me in the office in the morning. The calls and the notes came from people I knew outside of the television news area, and they revealed to me the depth of the division of which I had not been aware. They were from people who thought of themselves as Murrow loyalists in a fight to defend a fragile and critical tradition. I knew what we were doing in television news and was proud of it. These people didn't, and saw the television news branch as a kind of insidious destroyer of a lot of things important to them. They saw Murrow as the symbol, and they saw me, in that interview, as the youngster bought off and sent to destroy him.

I was upset, and I wrote Murrow a note. I told him of the reaction I had gotten, and said that if he shared the feeling that I had set out to undercut his credibility, I could only plead ignorance, not special interest.

I don't keep things around very well, and I wouldn't know where to lay hands on his answering note. But for obvious reasons it has stayed in my head, in essence, at least.

Don't worry about it, Ed wrote. I thought it was a very tough interview, which it should have been. I will defend my own reputation against fair questions, and that's all that happened. Let me tell you, he wrote, you'll go through worse things, and none of these people are speaking for me.

I suppose I showed that note to two or three people, none of them involved in that particular conflict. But it has been armor and shield to me ever since. We all, in an extremely professional and sentimental sense, walk in his shadow.

Occasion Two: On the second occasion in which Murrow entered my professional life, it didn't even involve a face-to-face meeting. I had been sent to Cuba in the spring of the last year of Fulgencio Batista's regime; Wendell Hoffman and I were there in April, at a time when "informed sources" (our "informed source" was a minor CBS News employee who—I believed then and believe now—actually worked for an intelligence agency) said that Fidel Castro, who had been camping up in the mountains of the Sierra Maestra for a couple of years, making mild and irregular forays, was ready for a major effort. There were a lot of us in Havana, quartered in the old Hotel Nacional, driving around at night in conspiratorial ways to interview Castro supporters, shooting a little dice in the almost empty casinos. Finally it became general inside knowledge that the next day was to be the day: an organized spontaneous uprising in Havana that would overthrow Batista and bring Castro to power.

We were up and out early that morning, with some nervousness. Our nervousness was directly related to the nervousness of Batista's police and militia. They were as well aware of the rumors as we were, and when you were stopped by them, you were highly aware of their uncertainty and their cocked revolvers. We toured the city, and it was, if anything, calmer than Havana usually was. We found nothing to film except one gas main that had been set on fire, perhaps by design, and was flaring rather dramatically at a downtown corner. No war. No insurrection.

We got back to the Nacional in early afternoon uncertain whether the film of one small street fire was even worth shipping to New York. But waiting for me was an urgent message to call New York and my immediate boss. I did, and the edited version of his message was that if I intended to spend my time in Havana in the sex resorts, ignoring war and turmoil, maybe I should get in some other line of work.

The problem was this: both major wire services in Havana at the time were staffed by very experienced reporters; both of the reporters had won Pulitzer prizes, as a matter of fact. They were understaffed to cover a war, and short of wars anyhow. So their coverage became a kind of competition, and on that day they had determined that there must be a war. The particular dispatch that had convinced my boss that I was cowering somewhere instead of being a reporter ran about like this: "As Fidel Castro's hidden revolution bloomed at last in Cuba, all employees of Havana's banks walked off the job today at noon, further making nervous the trigger fingers of President Batista's police."

That was read to me over the telephone, and I was constrained to be fairly forceful in my reply. There were two points, I said: Hoffman and I had been driving around Havana for five hours and there was no militant activity except the one damned gas main. And, as CBS News headquarters might not be expected to know but the Pulitzer Prize-winning wire-service reporter certainly did know, all Havana bank employees at the time walked off the job every day at noon and stayed away for three hours; it was a charming custom called a siesta.

It was not the first nor the last time that I caught members of my craft in something less than dedicated accuracy, of course; two other instances stick particularly in my mind. In 1965 I came in the office early for some broadcast connected with the funeral of Winston Churchill, and within a few minutes, around six o'clock—eleven or twelve, London time—the biggest of three wire services sent out an interesting item. Again a Pulitzer Prize winner was involved. The item read something like this:

> LONDON, Dec. 29 (AP)—Dwight David Eisenhower drove solemnly in the rain today and walked into Westminster Abbey to pay his last respects to his old wartime comrade, Winston Churchill. It may have been the rain, but some reporters thought they saw other signs of moisture on Eisenhower's face.

It as a little florid, but acceptable, I guess. Except that half an hour later the service sent out a BULLETIN MUST KILL, the strongest message a service can send its subscribers. The sense of the BULLETIN MUST KILL was: KILL ITEM A-47 MUST KILL EISENHOWER HAS NOT LEFT HIS HOUSE. I could see that reporter in some pub near the Abbey, checking the press releases detailing the day's events and saying, "Well, might as well get Ike Visits Bier piece out of the way," and going to the phone and doing it.

The second was an item in which I was involved in 1966 or 1967, when there was great tension between the Soviet Union and Czechoslovakia. In a last and, as it turned out, unsuccessful attempt to settle the matter without force, the Russians and Czechs met at a place called Cierno Nad Tisou on the weekend, and it was the lead item of my Sunday news. For an end-piece that night, in possibly misguided whimsy, I noted that only a few weeks earlier Premier

Kosygin of the Soviet Union had met with President Lyndon Johnson at a small college in New Jersey no one had ever heard of at a place called Glassboro. Isn't it interesting, I said, how history takes places like Sarajevo and Cierno Nad Tisou and Glassboro and makes them forever familiar? And isn't it strange that Cierno Nad Tisou, in Czech, means "Glassboro"?

Well, when I came in in the morning, that item was all over the radio. UPI had made a sidebar out of it—not crediting me, thank goodness, and even date-lining it as coming from Prague. Not until 11:30 a.m. did their BULLETIN KILL come out. Kill item A-43, it said; Czech authorities say Cierno Nad Tisou does not mean "Glassboro." It means "Black Town on the Tisa."

The thing to do if you are making a joke, I guess, is to put up a sign that says "joke." Most of your viewers will know anyhow, but you don't want to confuse some poor wire-service reporter. I concede it wasn't that much of a joke, either.

Obviously, we have digressed from Ed Murrow. The thing was, while I was in Havana basically for television, I was doing pieces for radio, too, including Ed's nightly fifteen-minute news, and he—in contrast to my over-eager television managers—liked my work in Cuba. A few months later he and Fred Friendly were going to do a *CBS Reports* on highway deaths, putting four correspondents at strategic locations over the Labor Day weekend. They had Murrow and Bill Downs and Bill Leonard; they needed a fourth man. Why, said Murrow to Friendly, why not give Reasoner a shot? It was my first chance to work with Friendly, my first real venture into documentary instead of day-to-day news. Murrow, who could have been sulking over the interview of more than a year before, made it possible. In collies, that's a character trait you call nobility.

The third of my Murrow connections came after he died. CBS, arranging a memorial broadcast, found out something I hadn't realized and neither had anyone else: the only time Ed Murrow ever talked on camera about himself and his philosophy was in a second interview with me, for the morning program *Calendar*, an interview we did after he had left CBS to become director of the United States Information Agency for John Kennedy. So I had the lovely, undeserved reward of being part of Ed Murrow's obituary.

I've always remembered one line from that interview. I had asked him what he thought of the star system that made people like him and Cronkite and Sevareid. He said it sometimes made him uncomfortable but he thought it had some advantages. The great thing, said Ed, is to keep this thing in perspective. Remember that just because your voice reaches halfway around the world, you are no wiser than when it reached only to the end of the bar.

6

1960

As noted, I had some despairing days in 1960, days in which I thought I had lost out in the Great Correspondents' Race, the Who-is-to-be-the-new-Murrow Sweepstakes, to that broth of a boy, Charles Kuralt. Oddly enough, parenthetically, until the end of that year we didn't see Walter Cronkite as an entry—we didn't see him in the role he made for himself in the next half-dozen years: not the second Murrow but the first Cronkite. I had some despair, but there was also a lot of fun-and-games that year. It was, as also noted, the year in which, unenthusiastically, I learned how to do radio and in the process was prepared for the Saturday- and Sunday-night news, *Calendar*, and my eventual role as the unseeded Mr. Cronkite's alter ego.

There were these other mini-sagas:

It was the only year of my career in which I did a lot of national political reporting, most of which reflected a reasonable amount of credit on me, but which also included the single biggest avoidable failure of my career.

It was the year of a major change in the hierarchy of CBS News—which included a giddy week in which, but for the good sense of others, I might have become a high executive.

It was the year of an exception to a personal rule—not rule maybe, conclusion or judgment: that in the sense of man-woman things my craft was not particularly romantic. In the years of story-chasing I had observed a lot of men on the road, some married, some not (that didn't seem to be the significant attribute). Some of them when they traveled made a lot of effort to meet women and to sleep with them. Some of them didn't. I didn't: for a lot of reasons it didn't seem to me to work. A lot of time the tryers worked very hard and got very tired and came home with an empty creel; most of the other times, when they were what they regarded as successful, what they wound up with struck me as vaguely depressing. Mornings after, it frequently struck *them* as vaguely depressing, too, and caused them to film things out of focus or ask the wrong questions. Anyhow, my rule, or conclusion, was that unless you tried very hard on the road, it was extremely unlikely that anything interesting would happen, and if you tried very hard, you lost a lot of sleep and it was highly unlikely that it would be very interesting anyhow. I had occasion to amend that conclusion in 1960. Sometimes things happen.

Shall we take up those items in the order listed?

I was assigned, at the beginning of 1960, to be the basic reporter covering Hubert Humphrey, who had a good chance to be the Democratic nominee for President. I had gone up to New Hampshire in January to cover the beginning of John Kennedy's campaign, but for the Wisconsin and West Virginia primaries and presumably right through the conventions and perhaps the fall campaign I was to be the Humphrey man. It seemed logical. I had known Humphrey since 1946, when he was the mayor of Minneapolis and I was a police reporter.

It was the first year when we began to worry about the problems of television coverage of campaigns. We had passed the novelty stage of being able to show pictures of candidates out in the field. We now realized that we could be patsies, merely furnishing an audience to listen to things the candidates wanted to say—and that we could be profoundly boring, showing one arrival, one speech, one at-the-factory-gate handshaking session after another without using television journalism to illuminate the people and the issues. We wanted to do more and to do it better; as of this writing, it remains an area in which progress has been minimal. A few people—Roger Mudd, for instance—have figured out how to do it. I thought I did all right in 1960, but I never got a chance to do it again.

I liked the job. In Wisconsin and again in West Virginia I was, in effect, competing against the correspondent assigned to Kennedy. Except that it was an intramural contest, it was like being back in Little Rock and trying to get a better story for CBS than Sander Vanocur was getting for NBC.

Kennedy, some of you will remember, was the one with the money. Humphrey's campaign alternately limped and lurched and occasionally, since Humphrey was the one with the verve, soared. But in West Virginia he was outspent. In those days campaign spending was very specific in West Virginia. It helped to have money for radio and television advertising, and money for direct mail, and money for an organization. But the general belief of informed West Virginians was that the most important use of money was for votes. I made a new friend in Charleston's Press Club the night I got there, and the next day we drove down to Morgantown, way to the south, and while my friend took care of some business, I wandered around and drank some beer and talked to people and found nothing to discredit her thesis, which was that if you wanted to vote for Kennedy in the Democratic primary, you could make five dollars for the favor. The old rate had been two dollars; it wasn't yet inflation in 1960, it was rising expectations. Five dollars, in 1960 and in West Virginia, was real money.

So Humphrey headquarters on election night was not a very jolly place. It was clear from the earliest returns that somebody had been giving away a lot of five-dollar bills—and not in behalf of Hubert Humphrey. Sometime around eleven o'clock I was in a bedroom of the hotel suite that served as headquarters, sitting in on a discussion between the candidate and Orville Freeman—then governor of Minnesota, I think, and later Kennedy's secretary of agriculture. Finally they reached a conclusion: at midnight they would concede the election. I asked Humphrey if he would mind if I used that for radio ahead of time—it would be a minor scoop, but you take what you can get. He told me to go ahead, so I left, made the radio report to New York, got mildly congratulated. Then a sudden depression hit me.

It is not an unusual thing. I have heard that sometimes between kidnapped and kidnapper, between hostage and captor, there arises a kind of dependency—a sentiment unexplained by a relationship which is basically antagonistic. It happens in just such a way between a reporter and any figure he is assigned to on a relatively permanent basis. The reporter is the hostage—in the case of a President or other major figure, one of many. He may or may not like his assignment, but he becomes extremely vulnerable to a sort of identification: if something happens to his tiger, he bleeds also. It doesn't—or at least it usually doesn't—affect the objectivity of his work; it just happens. It can go both ways, of course, and it can involve real friendship. I think of an instance in 1976 when Frank Reynolds, a reporter of great sensitivity and a man of deep principle and emotion, spent some months covering the pre-convention campaign of Ronald Reagan. It would be hard to picture two people with greater personal political differences than Frank and Reagan, but not only did Reynolds cover the Reagan campaign fairly, he and Reagan and Nancy Reagan became extremely close. On the night in Kansas City when Gerald Ford was nominated, Frank Reynolds cried—after he had done a final interview with the Reagans and was off the air, of course. I hope he doesn't mind my telling that, because it is something that has happened to most of us and—assuming it doesn't affect what you do on the air or in print—is kind of reassuring about reporters. I'm sure Reynolds thought that

Ronald Reagan would be a disaster as President of the United States—but he, in the process of trying to tell people honestly about Reagan, had come to love him and Nancy. I know. I thought Lyndon Johnson, overall, *was* a disaster as President, but I cried on the night in March 1968 when the old bastard said he would not run again. After we were off the air, of course.

I think the reason I say it is reassuring that reporters get involved that way does not in any way conflict with my other feeling that the great single qualification for a good reporter is detachment. You have to be detached, but you have to be able to love. Okay?

Anyhow, that in a minor way was what happened to me on primary-election night in West Virginia in 1960. What was in my mind was: Humphrey has lost here, things look bad for him; he's just going to send out a statement conceding the state—there isn't even any need for a film crew; I'll get up at five and see what the morning television report wants. I felt immeasurably and inexplicably physically weary, and I walked back to my hotel and went upstairs and went to bed.

I got up at five and called New York. An extremely cool Bill Crawford, my supervisor on the story, told me they didn't need anything. I was surprised, and argued. Look, he said, in effect, if the most important thing for you to do last night was shack up, that's your problem. Watch the morning report and you'll see why we don't need you.

What had happened, of course, was that Humphrey and Freeman and the rest of the top staff had not stopped talking and analyzing when I went off to get my scoop on radio—

and at 12:30 or so they had decided not only to concede West Virginia but to drop out of the campaign for the nomination. What I saw on television that morning was my intramural competition, the correspondent to Kennedy, covering the tears and the singing and all the poignance as Humphrey came downstairs and told that to the campaign workers. I had never blown a story quite so badly. I could have been fired, and it is extremely humiliating to have someone believe you deliberately goofed off when you don't even have the satisfaction of having deliberately goofed off. I suspect Crawford believes to this day I was engaged in hanky-panky. I wasn't, Bill.

ALL RIGHT, ITEM TWO: CBS television news came out of a series of conflicts and backings and fillings in the early 1950's, before I was there; by 1955 things seemed to have fallen into some kind of permanent organizational order: Fred Friendly and Edward R. Murrow had their own independent unit, but otherwise Sig Mickelson ran CBS News. Sig was a major pioneer and thinker in this business, and when he was himself on the scene, he was a good leader; his instincts on programming and journalism were unexcelled. But he had one problem: he had not been great at picking his staff. Then in 1956 NBC News put together the team of Chet Huntley and David Brinkley, and in two or three years the *NBC Evening News* had moved definitely out in front of CBS. This is not a situation anyone at CBS can tolerate very well, including Mr. Paley. The climax came in the conventions of 1960, when we just didn't look very good.

At Los Angeles, at the convention that nominated Kennedy, there was an attempt to make Cronkite and Murrow an anchor team, and it didn't work: in those days Cronkite did not work well in an equal relationship with anyone, and Ed was tired and unenthusiastic. Between conventions there was a high-level meeting in New York, chaired by Dr. Stanton, and the work of everyone who had been on the air at the convention was reviewed. In the case of floor correspondents, they were all rated either Good, Acceptable, or Bad. Only two were rated Good—me and, of course, Charles Kuralt. The machinery worked better at the Chicago convention that nominated Richard Nixon, but at the Dr. Stanton level there was still a real dissatisfaction with Sig and his staff. Sig realized that if he was going to stay, he had to make some changes of executives. I was on drinking-buddy terms with his chief assistant and had talked to him about what was wrong with the department from a correspondent's viewpoint, and it occurred to him and to me and then to Sig —mysteriously, it seems to me now—that I could replace John Day, the director of news, get along with Murrow and Friendly and Dr. Stanton, and restore CBS News in television to the pre-eminent place it had always had in radio.

There had been a moral issue in my business life once before—never mind it for this story—which had left me uncomfortable and suspicious of my own motives. I have to say that before agreeing to be Sig's candidate I went to my wife's priest to ask about the morality of my joining an effort which aimed at taking away the jobs of at least three executives who had been decent enough with me.

The priest said that I should examine my own conscience; obviously, ambition had a part in my decision, but if the main part of my desire for the job was concern for several dozens or hundreds of other CBS News people, the damage to the three or four executives could be justified. I decided my motives were relatively honorable. I suppose people usually do in cases like that. And I reasoned that someone was going to get rid of those men in any event; the question was whether in the process Sig would go, too. I hoped not.

It was a heady week, marked among other things as the only time in my CBS career when Don Hewitt, who was never much of a luncher, took me to lunch two days in a row. The climax was an interview with Dr. Stanton. Sig was not present, but a slender assistant named Richard Salant was. I didn't do very well in the interview, and I knew it. My plans and theories for turning the news department around were somewhat inchoate, and I didn't then and don't now know how to talk administrator's language.

The conclusion, of course, was that I didn't get the job. Instead, Sig did leave, along with his subordinates, and Richard Salant became president of CBS News, one of the best things that ever happened to the organization. He was, presumably, the man who vetoed me; I have suspected over the years that I should be heavily grateful to him for that, as well as for a lot of other things that came later. I went back to work and not lunching with Don Hewitt.

All of this happened sort of between two local disasters: the aircraft carrier *Constellation* burned in the Brooklyn Navy Yard and a week later a United Airlines DC-8 and a TWA plane collided in the air and a large part of the

United plane came to rest—looking, I remember, relatively intact—in a Brooklyn street. It looked like an airplane, but only one living person came out of it—a young boy who died later. We covered both those events eyewitness style with live mobile units. In those days that was an accomplishment.

The third item I mentioned was a charming tale of romance in Manila, and on second thought I don't think it belongs in this book. The woman in question went on to become a reporter herself and later wrote a novel.

As I said a few pages ago, even though the most important quality a reporter can have is detachment, you have to be able to love, too.

7

Calendar

I N THE LATE 1970's a thing began happening to me con-
sistently that had begun to happen ten years before. The
thing was this: if I went somewhere to make a speech, at the
reception before or from the crowd afterward a handsome
woman in her late thirties or early forties would come up to
me and say: "You helped me keep my sanity when the kids
were very small. What is Mary doing now?"

She would be talking about a television program called
Calendar, which ran for a half-hour, live, five mornings a
week for not quite two years from the fall of 1961 to the fall
of 1963. I was the host; an actress named Mary Fickett was
my co-host and my love.

I got to be the host in this way: the program had been
planned for some time to start in the fall; it was to be a
production of CBS News, but the idea was to get some
non-news correspondent to be its host—someone like Garry

Moore, maybe, or a younger Arthur Godfrey or Dave Garroway. They conducted a lot of auditions—Bill Leonard, at this writing the president of CBS News but then a producer, even auditioned himself—but no one was quite happy with anybody who tried out. There was to be a daily three-minute news segment on the program, and I had already been asked to do that when in late August they asked me if I would like to audition for the main role. The auditions were done in the evenings in an old building on 58th Street called Liederkranz Hall, a drafty structure which had been originally a German social club and which in the early days of television CBS had acquired. It had a sort of auditorium which was adaptable for studio use and some upstairs rooms. The popular belief was that by the time *Calendar* took it over, the old barn was held together by television cables and electrician's tape. I think that when CBS moved out in the mid-sixties and pulled out the cables and ripped off the tape, there was a certain disappointment among the technicians and stagehands that the building did not fall down; it had to be torn down.

Anyhow, the auditions were taped there in the evenings, and shown to executives and such the next day. They were simply structured: to audition, you conducted two interviews, since this was to be an interview show. The same two persons were interviewed by everyone trying out. It occurs to my conscience now that I hope they got paid. It couldn't have been much fun being interviewed by a dozen men of varying technique and competence, night after night. Of course, it wasn't much fun for us either.

I got the job, I think, because (a) in the interview with

one subject I happened to strike a note that had occurred to
no one else, and (b) because I happened quite honestly to
get into a lively argument with the other subject. And (c),
Mike Wallace's opinion to the contrary, I am a pretty good
interviewer.

Subject number one was an old black jazzman named
Noble Sissle. Something reminded me of my childhood
days, traveling summertimes with my father in an institution
called Chautauqua, a presumably entertaining and educa-
tional migrant tent-show that went around to Midwest small
towns and brought them small dramatic groups, inspirational
lecturers, cartoonists—and jubilee singers. Jubilee singers
were black gospel groups who sang things like "When I get
to heaven, gonna take off my shoes, gonna walk all over
God's heaven." Obligatorily, each group included a come-
dian, who would indeed during the final chorus take off his
patent-leather pumps and walk all over God's stage. I asked
Noble Sissle if he by any chance remembered, from the
they-all-got-rhythm-and-are-kind-of-cute-in-their-place era of
American race relations, whether he remembered jubilee
singers. "Remember them?" he said. "*Remember* them? I
was one." From then on we had a great time.

Subject number two was Betty Friedan. But wait a
minute. I'm sure that the thoughts and resentments and
insights that not much later made Betty Friedan the first
best-selling feminist of her time were already moving in her
head, but she wasn't selling feminism then, she was selling
education. You should remember that at that time feminism
was sort of like jubilee singers—something a few people
remembered with a kind of condescending affection: those

people in funny dresses who had managed to get the Nine-
teenth Amendment passed and since then had been grateful
and quiet except that in the 1920's they drank quite a bit of
gin. It was in the period when America was self-conscious
about Russia's pre-eminence in space, and Betty had attracted
some attention in her New Jersey community by organizing
Saturday classes in grade schools and high schools to help the
next generation of Americans catch up. I told her I thought
it was ridiculous. I asked her if anybody had polled the kids
on the question. I said that if I were one of her captive kids,
I would hate *her*, not the Russians. I said that if a school
system could not instill a reasonable amount of knowledge
in a twelve-year-old's head between Monday and Friday, it
was the system and the teachers who ought to take Saturday
classes, not the kids. In short, I was pretty mouthy, but so
was she, and it was lively, and it struck the evaluators that
it was the kind of thing they hoped *Calendar* would be—
literate without being pretentious, topical without being dull,
antagonistic without being rude, all of which the program
did turn out to be, which is why these handsome women who
at ten o'clock in those mornings of 1961 and 1962 and 1963
could take a half-hour off from changing diapers or washing
dishes keep coming up to me now and warming my heart.

So I was offered the job of being the host as well as
doing the news, and this immediately gave CBS News a
problem. *Calendar* had been designed to be a single-host
show, but in the nature of this kind of broadcast in commercial television, advertisers like a figure on the show to
read their commercials or at least introduce them in a

personal and approving way. CBS News correspondents could not read commercials. The solution was to change the format and get a co-host, a non-news person, a woman.

You will notice in these chronicles how often I have been a co-something. A surrogate for Cronkite. Me and Mike Wallace. Me and Mary Fickett. Me and Andy Rooney. Me and Howard K. Smith. And, briefly, me and Barbara Walters. I have gotten over worrying about what all this means and whether I should have inferiority feelings about it: things seem to work better that way. But I would like to note that this book is all mine (unless we decide to treat it as a pilot, recall it, and get a co-author).

Anyhow, it now became my turn to be both Noble Sissle and Betty Friedan and, night after night, stage interviews with women who had indicated they would like to be the co-host. It was, mostly, dull and deadly. I had anticipated, in a naïve, lubricious Iowa way, that some of the women might indicate that they thought a private audition with me might make their talents clearer, and in fact two of them did. I resisted the temptation because they weren't very tempting, which is, I suppose, why they tried to tempt. That's a sexist sentence, but remember it was they who—out of uncontrollable tradition, maybe—were being sexist first.

Then, on what in retrospect seems like the fiftieth night but was probably the fifth, a woman named Mary Fickett sat down in the chair opposite me. An actress who had gotten a lot of praise for playing Eleanor Roosevelt in *Sunrise at Campobello*, who had made a couple of movies. A tall and not startlingly beautiful woman—handsome, I think, like the women who watched *Calendar* later. And smart and quick and lovely and loving. It took only two or three questions for me to know she was the one, and the people in the control room felt the same way.

"You're a New Yorker," I said. "You don't *sound* like a New Yorker."

She said, "You should hear me when I chew gum."

Mary and I did roughly 450 broadcasts together. On the last broadcast we noted that meant we had each said "Good Morning" 450 times for a total of maybe twelve minutes; if we had omitted the good-mornings, we could have done two more interviews with gynecologists. We *did* do a lot of interviews with gynecologists—the Phil Donahue thing that some producers were more convinced even then was the stuff that women in the home and the small percentage of men with bad backs who were watching wanted to hear. I wasn't, neither was Mary, neither was our chief writer Andy Rooney nor our soon chief-producer Mel Ferber.

So we did a lot of things. We talked to authors—the other side of Phil Donahue, in case you thought what I said earlier was a crack at him—we talked to scientists, we talked to politicians, we talked to artists. We spent a weekend on one of those old Air Force radar platforms in the Atlantic; we went to London and Chicago and Washington and Boston and Zanesville, Ohio. We ended up one day on a bed in the studio with Salvador Dali as he (everyone, including Mary, knew it was going to happen except me) pulled out a can of aerosol-propelled shaving cream and made a sur-realistic work of art out of me.

Calendar

Here are some things about *Calendar*—one bad, several good.

It was my first experience at a kind of star status, and I wasn't perfect at it. I was sometimes temperamental. As a matter of fact, I was temperamental the first day of the broadcast. We had done a number of pretend shows, stressing the stated aim of the broadcast: that it would be literate and innovative (the producers-and-management theory) and that it might sometimes be bad but would contain no horseshit (my contribution). Then, on the Saturday or Sunday before our premiere, Roger Maris of the Yankees hit his sixty-first home run of the year, sort of breaking Babe Ruth's record. I say sort of, as I did on that premiere show, because he did it in a 162-game season; Ruth hit sixty in the previous mode of 154 games. Anyhow, I could have lived with the producers bringing in Maris—we always saw sports as being part of our province. But for the premiere of the most literate talk show ever done, with one of our initial guests Eric Sevareid, who do you think they got to talk about Maris' achievement? Not Maris. They got the guy from Brooklyn who was sitting in the bleachers and caught the ball, and his girl friend. I refused to do the interview, and, for the first time but not the last, Mary did it, graciously and without complaint. I was temperamental later: I declined to interview Peter O'Toole (he had been out all night and was disorganized) and I insulted Otto Preminger (as Wilson Mizner once said in another context and you may be thinking now: "in God's name, how?") and I insulted (the producers thought) some residents of Palm Beach when we did a week of broadcasts on how the other half lives. I was sometimes a temperamental bastard. But I also helped keep the horseshit off the program. End of bad thing, beginning of good things.

For me it meant the beginning of my association with Andy Rooney, who was the chief writer for *Calendar*'s first year—a long time for Andy to stick to anything—and its last week. We went on from there to do "Essay on Doors," "Essay on Bridges," "Essay on Women" (don't look that one up, please), "Essay on Chairs," "Essay on Hotels," "Essay on Whiskey," "Essay on War," and three programs filmed entirely from helicopters: "Bird's-eye View of America," "Bird's-eye View of Scotland," and "Bird's-eye View of California." He wrote, except for the endings, which he has a psychological block about (his idea of an ending was me standing there saying, "Well, that's our essay on bridges"); he wrote, and I read it off. Then when I left CBS, they didn't want to use "Essay on War" with my voice and no one else quite seemed to fit, so Andy bought the piece and put his own voice on it and sold it to Public Broadcasting. Once he found out he didn't need me, he became impossible. Andy Rooney is my best friend. We just don't talk to each other much. Well, that's my essay on Andy Rooney. That would be his ending to that paragraph. Mine would be that he, like Don Hewitt, changed the face and course of American non-fiction television.

Good thing: I learned to write little pieces that went with the time of the year or the subject of a given show.

Good thing: I worked with maybe the best assemblage of production and writing and executive talent ever assembled. I'd name them except I'd forget someone. They know who they are, and they wear the memory of *Calendar* like a medal.

Good thing: I met Mary Fickett. And, vicariously, all those great women who remember the show and ask me "What's Mary doing now?" Well, she's a star on a soap opera called *All My Children*, and I suppose the reason you don't know, kids, is that the babies are grown and you don't have to watch daytime television any more.

I'd like to append five pieces that maybe give some idea of *Calendar*'s flavor. The first is a piece I have used since, on *60 Minutes*, and which over the years has brought me more mail than anything else I ever did. Two are pieces that got me in trouble with the guests of the day—one a publisher's wife who thought I was full of it, one a piece I did after an interview with a representative of the American Cancer Society who was deploring smoking. He thought, very loudly, that I had sabotaged him. And, finally, just two of the sort of things we did.

CHRISTMAS DAY

So far as I know, all Christian denominations expect their members to go to church on Christmas Day. Sometimes it's the only time—or practically the only time—that some people do go to church—the Christmas and Easter Christians. I think sometimes the professional people in the church—the priests and ministers and the men who have to arrange extra seating—dislike this, and maybe in a way they resent Christmas, and the sentimentality that moves people on this day but which does not move them the rest of the year. It is this great sweep of emotion and the commercialism that goes with it, as a parasite bird with a blind rhinoceros, that leads some Christians to wish they would call Christmas something else—or maybe to wish that it had never been invented.

But it was invented—it did happen. And the basis for this tremendous annual burst of buying things and gift-giving and parties and near-hysteria is a quiet event that Christians believe actually happened a long time ago. You can say that in all societies there has always been a mid-winter festival and that many of the trappings of our Christmas are almost violently pagan. But you come back to the central fact of the day in the quietness of Christmas morning—the birth of God on earth. It leaves you with only three ways of accepting Christmas.

One is cynically—as a time to make money or endorse the making of it or to hope the economy does well.

One is graciously—the appropriate attitude for non-Christians in a Christian society who wish their Christian fellow citizens all the joys to which their beliefs entitle them.

And the third, of course, is reverently. If this *is* the anniversary of the appearance of the Lord of the Universe in the form of a helpless baby, it is a very important day.

It's a startling idea, of course. My guess is that the whole story—that a Virgin was selected by God to bear His son as a way of showing His love and concern for man—it's my guess that in spite of all the lip-service they have given it, it is not an idea that has been popular with theologians. It is a somewhat illogical idea, and theologians love logic almost as much as they love God. It is so revolutionary a thought that it probably could only come from a God who is beyond logic and beyond theology. It has magnificent appeal. Almost nobody has seen God and almost nobody has any real idea what He is like—and the truth is that among men the idea of seeing God suddenly and standing in the very bright light is not necessarily a completely comfortable and appealing idea.

But everybody has seen babies and most people like them. If God wanted to be loved as well as feared, He moved correctly here. If He wanted to know His people as well as rule them, He moved correctly here, for a baby growing up learns all about people. If God wanted to be intimately a part of man, He moved correctly here, for the experience of birth and familyhood is our most intimate and precious experience.

So it comes beyond logic; it is what Bishop Karl Morgan Block used to call a kind of divine insanity. It is either all falsehood or it is the truest thing in the world. It either rises above the tawdriness of what we make of Christmas or it is a part of it and completely irrelevant.

It is a story of the great innocence of God, the baby, God in the power of man, and it is such a dramatic shot toward the heart that if it is not true for Christians nothing is true, because this story reaches Christians universally and with profound emotion.

So if a Christian is touched only once a year, the touching is still worth it, and maybe on some given Christmas, some quiet final morning, the touch will take. Because the one message of Christmas is the Christmas story. If it is false, we are doomed. If it is true, as it must be, it makes everything else in the world all right.

BOOKS

I am a man of mild opinions, always eager to learn by listening to those better informed than I in various arts and sciences. This neutral and unprejudiced posture bends a bit, however, in the case of books. I have some prejudices here and propose to treat briefly on three of them.

First of all, I wish there would be a change from the present tendency of confusing case histories with novels or plays. A young boy or girl discovers that she or he is sensitive, that life is ineffable, that morals are flexible, that people have problems, and, instead of doing something kinetic about it like having a love affair or seeing a psychiatrist, sits down and writes a book. The basic confusion on the writer's part is between creation and therapy; the basic confusion on the critic's part is between sensitivity and writing talent. Writing talent is basically a built-in thing like the ability to spin a web in a spider, and when it is there and used, it produces that abstraction of experience, that mirror of life which is man's single greatest gift to man. When it is sensitivity rather than talent, it produces nothing of value except a doubtful sense of relief to readers who find that other people have the same problems.

Second, I wish writers would stop being creators of convention. It may seem paradoxical, but I think modern, forward-looking literature is more conventional these days than it was even in the Victorian era. It is conventional about different things, but the effect is the same: to substitute a literary tradition for experience. In the matter of sex, for instance, it is now just as conventional for two lovers in a book to have a wildly exciting time before marriage— sometimes before they've been introduced—as it was conventional for them not to in the old days, and it is just as misleading. What happens is that people who share with all of us the tendency to believe everything that is in print read these things, test them, find out it isn't that easy, and get so upset they go out and write another book, in which, of course, they pretend that it is.

And, finally, I wish readers would be a little less herd-like. If there is one rule I would recommend to any reader not specifically engaged in studying for an examination, it would be to read only what you like. It doesn't matter what it is: if you don't like it, don't read it. Reading is a pleasure or it is nothing. Following this rule will mean you are left out in the cold in a lot of literary discussions, where the basic standard for a book seems to be that it be unpleasant, but you can always go in the next room and pick up your copy of Ian Fleming or Richard Hughes or Rex Stout or Ernest Hemingway or Loren Eiseley and improve on most conversation anyway. Reading is about the only thing left in life that should be reserved for pure pleasure. Part of the danger here is the best-seller lists and various awards (with no disrespect meant to our guests today). A best-seller list or an award turns up some good things, but it also turns up things like *By Love Possessed*. And the same people who complain of the slavish attention that television programmers pay to ratings check off their progress through the best-seller lists of *The New York Times* with the devotion more properly paid to rosaries or a pre-flight procedure.

Read what you like. This can be anything from Edgar Rice Burroughs to Egyptology. But if reading is to achieve its purpose, it must be the most personal and rewarding thing in your life. Otherwise, it will never replace television.

SMOKING

I smoke too much myself and wish I didn't; I suspect that most adults who smoke wish they didn't, in spite of the undeniable fact that some smoking is among life's most rewarding pleasures. But the way most of us smoke is a prime symptom of our compulsive age: we smoke the way we drink or play golf or make money or chase trains; we act as if the measured passage of time is not enough, as if time had to be sweetened or seasoned or obscured to make the days shorten and blur, as if we would not like life if we stopped and looked at it clear, without a haze of smoke or alcohol or busyness.

But this is a problem of philosophy and not of medicine, and it seems to some people that if you quit smoking because you are afraid of lung cancer, you may be quitting for the wrong reason. It's been fairly widely held for a long time that smoking was a bad thing; most of us would regret the day a child begins because it means so little to him till he starts and is then a small monkey on his back forever; most of us find some fault with the advertising that promotes smoking among the young. But smoking is a pleasure, one of the real ones, and if you take the position that it is not immoral, then you should not have to quit for health reasons unless you are sick. The idea of trying to outguess life, to avoid everything that might conceivably ever injure your life, is a peculiarly dangerous one, I think; pretty soon you are existing in a morass of fear and you have given up not only cigarettes, prime beef, good butter, fine whiskey, spinach, tennis, sleeping on your side, riding without seat belts, air travel, train travel, your chiropractor —maybe, next month, love.

A man makes a sort of deal with life. He gives up things because they are undignified or piggish or immoral; if life asks him to cringe in front of all reasonable indulgence, he may at the end say life is not worth it. Because for the cringing he may get one day extra or none; he never gets eternity. If eternity exists, it is available not on the basis of how hard you hold to life but how generous you are with it.

We have noted that some governments and some health agencies think the business of making and selling cigarettes is so dangerous it should be regulated, and this may be true; it ought to be possible to find out if it is true, and certainly any desirable action should not be withheld because of economics. But on an individual basis, what you do about smoking may be about like what you do about any other personal behavior: something you should not decide on the basis of fear.

It may not be wise or manly to act only to stay alive: the odds are that you will die anyway.

TOILET TRAINING

Every once in a while someone remembers that part of the aim of this program is to be of service to women and we schedule someone who takes a depressing view of how to get along with your husband, or someone who is for or against summer camps, or someone who has radical new ideas on education, like, for instance, that children should begin with calculus and work backwards to the multiplication tables.

But in some fields I have made it clear that I am the expert. For instance, the matter of toilet training. A brief survey has shown that last weekend there were more hours spent at social gatherings in the United States discussing toilet training than were spent discussing Elizabeth Taylor and Eddie Fisher, possibly because it's a less predictable subject.

In modern novels about suburbia, writers usually indicate that this concentration on talk about children and their habits is pretty bad and tends to make husbands have lunch with their secretaries because their wives are dull. It may be that these writers have run into a different group of secretaries than I have, or that they stay in the country all the time and get their ideas about secretaries from the movies, because my personal feeling is that you just can't beat a rousing, no-hold-barred discussion of how to get a child out of diapers.

How David Susskind has missed it so far I can't understand, and if he would like me to be on the panel, I'd be delighted. You are bound to get as many well-thought-out and well-defended theories as there are participants, and the general conclusion is usually that some children are different from others. Some of ours certainly are. My fifth girl had us worried, frankly. We were beginning to think of her eventual college in terms of an understanding housemother. There didn't seem to be any neurosis about it. She just didn't care, and then we went away for two weeks and when we came back she had trained herself. Sort of. I guess a psychologist would say she was getting even with us for going away, and I think that's grand.

Number five in untrained days just didn't care. Maybe none of us should.

WEATHER

It's so beautiful up in the country these mornings that it's worth getting up early to look around. Seventeen commuters in my town who had put their houses on the market and decided to move back into town canceled their plans after yesterday's sunrise; they absorbed enough radiance to last them until Daylight Savings starts and they can get their charcoal grills out of the cellar.

What it is is one of those two or three times a year that not only make commuting worthwhile, or farming, or any other status that brings you up against the hard facts of nature, but, maybe more important, make life in a temperate zone, a climate of harsh and dramatic change, more attractive than anything else in the world.

Sometimes about this time of year we get a real warm day—and we did, Sunday—and then it gets real cold again that night—and it did, Sunday night—and then the wind comes up gusty and fresh from the northwest and it blows away the cobwebs and vacuums the air and freezes the little puddles on the grass so fast you get ripples in the ice. The air is like a tonic and you can see a million miles, even in New York, and you wouldn't live anywhere else for anything.

In Manila, in the tropics, they tell the story of the man who came home from the office one day after ten years, sat down on his porch looking out over Manila Bay, took one sip of his drink, said, "Oh, no, not another damn beautiful sunset," and went inside and shot himself. Nobody in the temperate zones ever shot himself on account of the weather; at least, not on account of the monotony in the weather. The weather here keeps you interested, for or against, and sometimes, like yesterday or today, it can be intoxicating.

In case we have another day of it, the thing to do is to be outside, or by a big window, at just about 6:15 in the morning, in this longitude at least. Position yourself on high ground, with the ground sloping away from you sharply to the east and then climbing again; the west bank of a ravine does nicely. Right then you're looking at the black and white of the world: the other side of the ravine is absolutely black—there could be a city or a pride of lions or seven houses of neighbors hidden there—and the sky above the line of the hill is a bright, silvered white—no color at all. And then, before you get too cold to watch, the pink and orange of the sun comes, and the black of the hillside rolls down from the top, down to the river, and there are no lions there at all, but the empty branches of the trees are so clear you think you've never seen a tree before.

And then you go milk the cows or catch a train or cook the cocoa or whatever it is you do at 6:25 in the morning. And whatever it is you do, it's easier.

8

LBJ

I WAS ASSIGNED to succeed Dan Rather as White House correspondent in February 1965. I think Fred Friendly's theory was to give Dan, up from Texas only a couple of years, some seasoning in the London bureau, and to give me a job where I would learn about Washington and where I would have to work.

I had mixed feelings. I had already developed a kind of distaste for Washington's insularity. And I wasn't particularly sure it was a job I would be very good at.

A note or two about White House work: in the first place, it is not all that glamorous. What it is, really, is the world's most important police beat. It has the same characteristics as any police headquarters: reporters and technicians sit around most of the time, gossiping and lying; some of them drink too much at lunch. You are dependent both for your news and for the length of your working day on the whims of one man—you go home when his press secretary says there is a "lid," which means he does not expect anything more newsworthy to happen that day. The highlight of your day may have been standing in disorganized serried ranks in the Rose Garden for an hour, waiting for the President to speak three minutes about the virtues of American youth as he honors the 4-H boy and girl of the year. It is like any police beat: years can go by and you barely note them and suddenly you are an old fellow guarding your favorite chair in the lounge and grousing about the food on the last trip and reminiscing about the days when a press conference was Franklin Roosevelt calling a dozen people in for a friendly chat. I was surprised to realize, and then not surprised, that, except for the wire services and a few good newspapers and the broadcast networks, the quality of the White House press corps is not high. I think if you are an editor on a run-of-the-mill paper that wants the prestige of a White House staff byline, it is the kind of job you send the publisher's cousin to if he has been messing up the obituary desk.

Not that there is no way to be a good White House reporter. The best two I saw were Robert Pierpoint, also there for CBS, and Charles Roberts, then there for *Newsweek*. To be a good White House reporter, you don't guard your chair in the lounge; you get to know the secretary of the National Security Council. You don't take too many drinks at lunch, you have a business-like sandwich with the overworked assistant press secretary. You keep copious and detailed notes on everything that happens. So that when the briefing *does* come, when the additional men are sent to

Vietnam, you know what you ought to know about how the thing came about, and what questions to ask, and who to talk to after the formal announcement. It's beat work, and I am not a good beat reporter, as opposed to Pierpoint or Roger Mudd. Especially since I was still required to be in New York two or three days a week, Pierpoint saved me.

But I think I did a good job in a principal requirement, which was understanding and reporting Lyndon Johnson. I got along well with him, which some of my peers would say was prima-facie evidence that I wasn't tough enough. I don't agree, obviously. The time that I was there coincided with the final plunge into our terrible mistake in Vietnam, and I think we reported that accurately, reflecting the President's puzzlement as he slid deeper and deeper into a situation which he knew meant his political death and the end to his dreams of going down in history as a great President of all the people.

He was, as David Halberstam made clear in his book *The Best and the Brightest,* to some extent a prisoner of the elite corps of advisors he had inherited from John Kennedy. These men were not villains—they were just terribly wrong and, with a couple of exceptions, completely unable to consider the possibility that they were wrong. McGeorge Bundy was the prime example. He was one of those American patricians who could make a midwesterner like myself —and maybe a Texan like Lyndon Johnson—feel that your fingernails were dirty the moment you walked into his presence. At the same time he could look at a row of facts with dirty fingernails and simply not see them. Mr. Johnson was also, I think, somewhat overly impressed with the military, and their charts and graphs and colonels with long pointers explaining them. Parenthetically, I think Presidents Kennedy and Nixon were, too; all three of those men had been junior officers in World War II and perhaps they were fascinated by being deferred to by generals and admirals, bemused by graphs and slides. It is one of the advantages of having a soldier President: Dwight Eisenhower had been up to his navel in generals and admirals for half his life and he could take or leave alone their advice. So he could make the decision not to help the French in Vietnam in 1954, not to fight for Quemoy and Matsu, and if he had been President in the first half of the sixties, we might be around fifty thousand lives richer, and immeasurably less torn apart.

But we didn't have Eisenhower, we had Lyndon Johnson, a giant confidence-man of a President in many ways, but, from the standpoint of a reporter who got along with him, inexhaustibly rewarding. This is the glamor side of the White House police beat—if you represent a major entity like CBS News, you get considerable private time with the President, along with White House dinners and other things calculated to turn your head. Being asked your opinion about United States policy by the President or the Secretary of Defense is seductive stuff. All you can do is remember that they are asking you because you are CBS News, not because of any intrinsic charm or knowledge. James Kilpatrick, the conservative columnist and commentator, put it very well in a piece when he was editor of the Richmond, Virginia, *News-Leader*. "Just because you sup at the tables of the great," he warned journalists, "don't forget you are the same inky wretch who begged last night and will tomorrow for

crumbs at the kitchen door." Not enough Washington reporters have read that, or remembered it.

Anyhow, we had this big, ebullient, manic-depressive
Texan, who never would have made it to the presidency on
his own and whose realization of that affected his bigness
and ambition and inner complexities. This is not a biography
of Lyndon Johnson, but he is the only President I ever knew
with any degree of intimacy, and he obviously impressed me.

He had to the end a suspicion of the East, and of New
York, a suspicion that was the other side of the coin of the
respect that made him listen too long to the balderdash of
people like Bundy and Henry Cabot Lodge. He thought of
New York as a strange and closed-in place where he would
never be welcome. When I had been away from the White
House once for a week or so, he called me aside: "I suppose,"
he said, "you've been up there drinking old-fashioneds at that
Twenty-one Club." There was no practical way to convince
him that most reporters don't drink at "21" very much, and
that the people who do drink at "21" gave up old-fashioneds
as the drink of choice sometime around 1937. He was misted
in his stereotypes, and they included not only New York but
the Asians and the military and the persuasive intellectuals
of John Kennedy's Boston.

In December of 1965 I was in Austin because the President was spending the Christmas holidays at his ranch. CBS
planned an hour-long review of the Vietnam story for the
end of the year, and I was asked to see the President if
possible and be prepared to voice the White House view of
how things were going. I asked the press secretary—Bill
Moyers then—if I could get fifteen minutes with the Presi-

dent to make sure I understood the White House view. The requested fifteen minutes turned into an afternoon and evening at the ranch and included a moment that has stuck with me.

Bill, and Mrs. Johnson, a secretary, and I, were riding with the President in his Lincoln convertible—the Johnsons in front, Bill and I and the secretary in the back. We were taking one of those aimless drives that seemed to relax Mr. Johnson—into Johnson City to look at a building he was remodeling, over the back roads, seventy-four miles an hour down the state highway. In late afternoon we stopped by a grove of what pass for trees in that part of Texas, and the President craned around from the front seat.

"Look," he said, "I think we're reasonably safe at the moment—the radio's quiet, the Secret Service station wagon behind us is quiet. I think Bill and you are both loyal Americans." I tried to look loyal. "We're out here in the middle of nowhere. You be President. Tell me what you'd do."

I said, "Bill?" and Bill said, "Harry?" simultaneously. And then I waffled. "Mr. President," I said, "I'm sure you know a lot of things I don't. The only thing I would say, as a former non-com, is that I would be suspicious of the military and what they tell me."

We resumed our aimless, therapeutic driving. At a family dinner that night Mr. Johnson came back to the subject without warning as he slurped his soup.

"Harry says I should be suspicious of the military," he said. "Listen, I could tell you things the military has sug-

LBJ

gested to me and I've turned down that would _curl_ your
hair."

That was the third side of the coin of Lyndon Johnson,
if I can stretch that metaphor past its breaking point—a very
real innate shrewdness and judgment of what was possible.
Too bad, in foreign affairs, he didn't have more confidence
in what he instinctively knew.

9

Friendly

AT THIS WRITING, fourteen years after his last formal connection with CBS News, I suppose the strangest thing about Fred Friendly is that he has mellowed. His old and close friends saw it happen bit by bit, but the colleagues and servitors like myself who saw—and see—him only from the outside and only once in a great while in person find it hard to believe. He was such a great flamboyant in our professional youth, such a factor of both inspiration and disruption, that it is hard to believe what we see now: the man heard from only on lofty and sometimes abstruse First Amendment issues, the quiet scholar at Columbia, the senior statesman observing insufficiencies in journalism with wry and detached criticism in *The New York Times* or some academic journal instead of shouted rages and pleading histrionics in the newsroom or the screening room or cutting room.

Let me put the bones of his history in a paragraph. After Sig Mickelson was eased out of the news presidency, Richard Salant was made president. He immediately began to put together the frame and the spirit that led to the dominance and excellence of CBS News for two decades, and why anyone—presumably Mr. Paley was "anyone" in decisions like that—would want to replace him was, on the face of it, beyond an answer. I assume the answer had to do with a vague feeling of discomfort and inappropriateness: Salant was not a journalist, he was a lawyer; he had been highly involved in corporate activities that I assume were close to lobbying; he was relatively unknown to the rank and file of the news organization.

For whatever the reason, Salant gave up the job in 1964, and CBS announced that Fred Friendly had become president of CBS News. In a book he wrote, Fred credits me with one of the first comments on his appointment: "My God," he quoted me as having said in an early-morning conversation with him after the appointment was announced, "the lunatics have taken over the asylum." I had been indeed flattered to get one of the first telephone calls from him, but what I said was: "You know, Fred, you are an executive in the sense that Willie Sutton is a banker." The story tells you something about Fred if you had worked with him in the preparation of films: the determination to do it over, to labor and revise and polish, until you get it right. Fred was never dishonest in journalism; he just refused to believe that there was not somewhere, in some overlooked roll of film, in some mislaid section of the critical interview, that somewhere, legitimately, was the exact phrase, the perfect cut-away, the unsubstitutable picture. He, when he wrote his book, had found what he wanted me to say, what he was sure expressed my best perception better than what I had actually said. Again, not dishonest—I probably did say what he quoted, in some obscure, forgotten roll of the long mental films of our association.

Fred was out of radio in some place like Providence, Rhode Island. He became closely identified with Edward R. Murrow after the big war. They did several record albums together called *Hear It Now*, which were highly successful and evocative of the real sounds and feelings of the 1930's and '40's. As Murrow stepped tentatively into television, it was only natural that Fred would go with him and that their first great achievement would be a weekly program called *See It Now*.

The years have clouded the professional perception of *See It Now* and made it seem more than it was. But it was enough without any gilding. It was relatively fearless, as when it was the first major organ of mass journalism to stand up to Senator Joseph McCarthy and articulate the growing public distaste for the witch-hunting of the early fifties. It was innovative: it did as much as any program to break ground in what television could do for documentaries, in the realization that longer pieces on television had to be different from *Nanook of the North*, that the evening news had to be different from newsreels. It couldn't have been done without the prestige and credibility of Murrow, but it probably could not have been done either without the driving force and will to excel and educate that Friendly brought to it. The pair went on from *See It Now* to *CBS Reports*, the great weekly series.

Friendly had a kind of fiefdom, exempt largely from either budgetary or editorial control from CBS News executives. He had the exemption partly because of Murrow, partly because it was believed he had a pipeline to Dr. Stanton, the president, whose influence in CBS then was almost as great as Mr. Paley's, and partly because Fred wouldn't have it any other way. He was an instinctive rebel against any control, apart from his own, over any enterprise he was associated with. It was this perception that gave me immediate doubts about the decision to make him president. A great producer can be completely selfish in fighting for his own project; a great executive has to apportion and deny. Fred could and did haunt—sometimes, to producers and correspondents and film editors, that seemed like the literal word—every step of the production of a *CBS Reports* episode. But there was no way the president of CBS News could keep day-to-day track of everything that was going on. Fred had to face that, but he never liked it, and I think it contributed to the unconscious goal set in his mind. He was looking for a confrontation of the creative kind that used to make his productions so good, but executives are supposed to avoid confrontations so that the people under them—the Friendlys—can do their work without let or hindrance.

The climax came rather quickly. CBS reorganized itself, putting a group president in charge of all broadcasting activities, supervising the television network and the radio stations. This meant that on the organizational chart Fred could no longer pick up the phone and call Dr. Stanton or Mr. Paley directly: his pipeline now went first to a man he didn't have much in common with named Jack Schneider. Schneider in turn felt an obligation to rather quickly assert his authority over this long-independent man—not to emasculate CBS News, I think, but for the confidence in the chain of command that a man like Schneider would feel was necessary. Richard Salant, at least as uncompromising and highly principled as Friendly, could live with that: he understood corporations and understood how to get good things accomplished without provoking interior chaos. Fred didn't, and he picked what was practically the first opportunity for confrontation. In the event, he was wrong. It was the case of the hearings over Vietnam policy in the Senate Foreign Relations Committee in 1966. Fred wanted the network to broadcast them live. Schneider didn't, except on a selective basis for important sessions. Schneider's position was this: he was perfectly willing to allot a half-hour of prime time every night for a digest of that day's meetings, but he saw no point in pre-empting all of a daily schedule for proceedings which were for a large part dull or self-serving or repetitive. A carefully monitored and edited and analyzed version, on the air at a time of triple the potential audience, would serve professional responsibility better, Schneider thought. I think he was right; I think Fred was spoiling for a fight. He made the question an ultimatum to Dr. Stanton and Mr. Paley, and he lost. Salant came back.

All right—Fred Friendly and me.

. . .

THE FIRST TIME I ever worked for Friendly was in September 1959 on the *CBS Reports* story on Labor Day traffic. Until he left in 1966, except for the two years of the program called *Calendar*, I worked more for and with him than for anyone else. But we were, I think, never completely friends; I never completely won his respect. He thought I was lazy, and said so on a couple of occasions, not to me. He kept trying, through the years, to reform me: to instill in me the single-minded dedication to fire-in-the-belly journalism that he had. The thing was, he was fair enough not to argue with my productivity: in those years of utility-infielder status, of my being a kind of designated hitter, I did more work than any other correspondent. He just thought I didn't look tired and pressured enough in the doing.

When your boss is not only your boss but perhaps the most respected producer in broadcast journalism, it doesn't do you any good in the organization to have him characterize you as lazy, because other people believe it. Bill Leonard, an ex-correspondent who wanted to be the next Fred Friendly, believed it, for instance, and in his case that belief was part of the reason I left CBS in 1970. Gordon Manning, another boss of mine, believed it until I left, he once said, and was then surprised when he had to find three correspondents to do the things I had been doing.

I don't remember the first time I saw Friendly in the flesh; I suppose it was during my first assignment to *CBS Reports*, the one that Ed Murrow recommended me for. But I remember first impressions. He was a distinctive-looking man and, in a strange way, rather attractive. Like Roger Mudd, he gave the impression of being larger than he was.

In both cases it is the size of the head and hands and feet, like a Labrador pup that has not yet grown into the dimensions of its extremities. Fred had an extremely rare charm. Even after I knew him better, even when I believed I had good reason not to trust his concern for me, he could take me to lunch and in a few minutes convince me to do something I didn't want to do.

Why wasn't I his kind of man? Why did he think I was at least lazy and perhaps, as the French say, not *sérieux?* Well, there are two possible reasons that I have brooded about over the years. The first is deductive and defensive. I think, in a way he may never have realized consciously, Fred was determined never to be saddled with another Murrow, with a correspondent whose influence and personality were stronger than his own. This is a common and understandable feeling among producers. I think a lot of times they seem to themselves to have done most of the creating and then resent seeing the man on the screen get the credit. But in Fred's case, for all his love for Murrow, seeing him leave was not an unalloyed sadness: Fred was now his own man and he could make all CBS News excel in his image. He didn't want another Murrow—or a Cronkite, or a Reasoner.

The other possible reason for his attitude toward me has of course occurred to you.

Maybe I am lazy.

ONE FRED FRIENDLY STORY, and I offer it with the free admission that I cannot document it. That's all right—at worst it's like that quote Fred used from me in his book: it *ought* to be true if it isn't, and somewhere on some roll of film you could find it.

The thing is, there has always been, along with a saintly disregard of creature comforts—even his own—there has always been, with Fred, a kind of prudishness. Not prudishness—naïveté, maybe. Anyhow, CBS News was doing a major documentary on abortion a dozen or so years ago, produced by David Lowe, Senior, a fine producer, now dead. David came back from a field trip connected with the story and was chatting with Fred. "I ran into a fascinating story in Los Angeles," David said, "but I don't think it's anything we can use. It's just fascinating. I met this well-to-do lady in Los Angeles who wanted an abortion." I should note that this conversation was at a time when abortion was still illegal in most cases. "There was," David went on, "no particular problem. Her doctor was cooperative, and sent her to a trustworthy man in Mexico City. He performed the operation, packed the wound, and sent her back to Los Angeles, with instructions to go to a certain doctor in downtown Los Angeles in two days to have the packing removed. When she got home, the lady had some reflections. Her doctor in Beverly Hills knew all about the business—why should she go to some stranger to have the packing taken out? So she went to her own doctor, and he took out the packing and everything was fine. The only thing was that the packing contained about eight ounces of pure heroin."

Fred thought a minute. "You're right," he said, "that is

fascinating—but I don't see how it fits in our piece. Incidentally, isn't that an awful lot of heroin to kill the pain?"

One more Friendly story, documentable: in 1966 or '67, CBS News produced a one-hour documentary on homosexuality. In looking at a relatively final version, Fred had a comment.

"You know," he said to correspondent Mike Wallace, "it occurs to me I don't know, and I'll bet a lot of people don't know, exactly what homosexuals *do*. We ought to tell people."

So Mike went to a doctor who had been a consultant on the film, and, before a film camera, asked him, "Doctor, just what do homosexuals do?" In brief but graphic detail, the doctor told him. Mike showed the film to Fred. The subject was never mentioned again.

Incidentally, that was only fourteen or fifteen years ago, but, given the subject, the film had to be screened ahead of time for CBS affiliates. The narration was so circumspect you would find it hard to believe it was the same Mike Wallace we know and love. Two stations, I think, declined to show it—one in Arkansas, one in San Francisco. Probably for different reasons.

And would you believe that a film on homosexuality, made fourteen years ago, could go on for a full and frank hour and never once *mention* female homosexuality? Progress, or at least change, has come fairly rapidly in some areas, hasn't it?

10

Combat

I HAD MANAGED, as I suppose most Americans of my generation had managed in spite of World War II and the Korean War, to reach the age of forty-four without hearing a shot fired in anger at myself. That may not be strictly true, I guess, on reflection. On several occasions when I crawled the Infantry combat-training course in 1943, the training lieutenant certainly looked angry as he fired at me. But he was bound by honor and the fear of court-martial to keep from hitting me and I had confidence in his marksmanship, so the feeling as the bullets whistled above my fundament (he thought it was too *high* for both decorum and my future survival) was one of mild exhilaration, not fear.

I had heard bombs a few blocks away in Saigon in 1953, and random shots during the troubles in Manila in 1951 and 1952, but there was no feeling of someone personally shooting or bombing *me*. That I saved for 1967, and after that for a while it seemed to happen fairly often.

In 1953, as you may remember, Vietnam was still under the nominal control of the French. I had arrived in Saigon on a mission for the United States Information Agency and its regional publications. I spent a night in a fortified hamlet, which was the 1953 example of a light at the end of the tunnel; with American aid the French and the Vietnamese government had established some experimental villages, heavily guarded. The theory was that loyal farmers from many kilometers around would come in there at night, leaving the fields and the roads to the Viet Minh. I had an uncomfortable and nervous night, but heard no hostile sound.

The next night, back at the old Hotel Majestic in Saigon, I had some drinks with three or four American officers including the captain who had been my escort in the hamlet. I suppose they were a substantial percentage of the American military then in Vietnam. There weren't even any "advisors" then; these and their few colleagues were merely expert guides to the French in the use of the American weapons then being furnished. They were, I guess, like the "training officers" sent to El Salvador.

They were bright and attractive young men; the highest rank at the table was major. They were frustrated and contemptuous of the French. What kind of tactics was it, they asked, to abandon the countryside each night at sunset, so that the enemy could without fear or hazard do whatever he wanted in the way of re-supply and movement? How accurate was it to maintain that you controlled Route 1 if you had to reopen it behind heavy armored units every morning? It was, said the young officers, a joke, a symptom of the French lack of will, of the sapping of French resolve that had begun at Verdun and ended at Vichy. On a fourth brandy-and-soda, the major summed up the attitude of the career American military—the career American military who had seen Vietnam and knew what was going on.

"It's the French," the major said. "It's the French. The Viets are perfectly all right if someone would lead them. Give us control and a few thousand special troops and we could wind this up in six months."

I was impressed but not convinced.

It was a long time before the American military lost their optimism. This is to their credit. By definition, military men have to be ready to go optimistically ahead; pessimists don't win wars. Eleven years later, in North Carolina, I talked to another major, a Green Beret headed back for his third tour in Vietnam. Even by then, just after the incident and resolution called the Tonkin Gulf, things looked pretty bad. The unexpert feeling, after I watched the French despairing of it, that this was a war nobody could win had been steadily reinforced. I said to the major that it was too bad we were getting involved with ground troops. "Are you crazy?" he said. "Can you imagine a better way and place for training? We need it. It's wonderful." He was not a bad man, or a war-lover. He was a professional. The worst casualty of the Vietnam war may have been the spirit and confidence of men like that. They are as yet, in an imperfect world, indispensable. We just asked them to do things for us that we should have not have asked.

By the time I went back to Vietnam for CBS News in 1967, we were fully in it. As a White House correspondent, I had covered Lyndon Johnson as he changed—changed knowing it and hating it and despairing of it and helpless to stop himself—as he changed from the President who got the voting-rights act passed for John Kennedy's memory to the President who got us into Vietnam. I've discussed Mr. Johnson elsewhere in this book, but this is the place to mention his reaction to my trip. At that time I was the anchorman on the *CBS Sunday News*, also an experience discussed elsewhere. CBS News by then was spending a million dollars a year on the Saigon bureau; relatively junior correspondents like Morley Safer and Jack Laurence were making reputations there, as their seniors had done in Europe and Korea. As part of the tactics that kept three or four of these reporters there on year-long tours, and some-times one- or two-year renewals, CBS also liked to have one senior correspondent there at all times, on rotating three-month tours. It was a voluntary matter, and I had been volunteering regularly since the beginning of 1965. I knew Asia, I contended; I had been in Saigon and even in Phnom Penh, which in 1967 was just a funny name where that funny prince who played the clarinet was sort of in charge. So, I contended, I was a logical choice for a three- or maybe six-month assignment. But by then I had become the utility infielder of CBS News. I had the *Sunday News*, and I was the regular substitute for Walter Cronkite, and I was the man available for sudden specials, or for the series of hour shows on Vietnam that we had begun, and for a series called *Who, What, When, Where, Why* that was—two years before *60 Minutes* began—the first CBS News prime-time broadcast since Edward R. Murrow did *CBS Reports* to have a regular *host*, a personality who might, God forbid, thought CBS News management, become a *star*, and therefore a personality problem. So I was put off with kind words for my dedication and bravery. It may be that Fred Friendly and after him Richard Salant thought there was something suspicious about this constant volunteering. In any event, I could not get a Vietnam assignment.

But in the late summer of 1967 Vietnam was having an election campaign. Nguyen Van Thieu and Nguyen Cao Ky —the marshal who wore the black jumpsuit uniforms—and a few others were contending in an American style for the presidency. It should be noted that they took to American political styles about the way their armies took to American military methods: it looked all right, but there was a certain substance missing. CBS News decided to do a half-hour on the campaign, and I was asked to go over and do the reporting. It was understood that in the time I was there I would also be allowed to cover a few spot stories on the war.

So on one Sunday night at the end of the news broadcast I told the audience that I would be missing for three Sundays and that Mike Wallace would be filling in. We had established, as noted elsewhere, a pattern of doing something at the end of that broadcast, when we could without forcing it, that was a little different—poignant, maybe, or witty, we hoped—and so to the bones of the announcement I added: "I haven't been in Vietnam since 1953, so I'll have to study up on it. I understand the French have left."

A moment or two after we were off the air the telephone

rang. It was Mike with a severe reprimand. How, he wanted to know, did I get the consummate nerve and bad taste to speak lightly of a news story where Americans were dying, where freedom was at stake? I told him how, and he wished me well and rang off. A moment after that the secretary got another call. The White House is calling, she said, and the President wants to speak to you. Knowing that Mike Wallace was in town, near a telephone, and in a puckish mood, I was suspicious, but when I picked up the phone those accents were unmistakable. Nobody ever convincingly imitated Lyndon Johnson except John Connally, and he presumably doesn't mean to.

"Harry," said the President, "when you going to Vietnam? You got time to come down here first and I'll *brief* you?" I said that I would make time, and when would it be convenient?

"Let me see," said Mr. Johnson. "I got the Germans tomorrow and that English prime minister Tuesday—he wants some money. Make it Wednesday."

So my briefing on the war began with the man who was leading it. He was heavier than he had been while I was at the White House, and somber, and breathing thickly, as he tended to do when he was trying to convince someone of something he perhaps was not sure of himself. He told me—as he had in 1965 and 1966—of his efforts, public and private, to get the North Vietnamese to make some kind of compromise that would let us get out, if not with a coonskin, at least with some semblance of honor. And he, at my request, sent me over to see Secretary of Defense McNamara for a further briefing. It was in McNamara's office that I realized that the holdover coalition of intellectuals who, collected by John Kennedy, had advised Mr. Johnson and the country into the war was eroding; Bill Moyers had left by then, and Robert McNamara was obviously tortured. Only McGeorge Bundy and Dean Rusk and Walt Rostow and a few others held firm. I only had one real question for McNamara: could he, if he had to face up to a situation where he realized that a position he had long defended and which had had incalculable consequences for the country had been wrong—could he, in such a situation, change his policy, admitting to the waste and idiocy and failure?

"That," said McNamara, "is the question I ask myself every morning at the shaving mirror."

Anyhow, a day or so later I was on my way back to Asia for the first time since 1960. After a shaky beginning when something went wrong with our airplane, and after a night in Tokyo, getting there was easy enough. I paid my call on Barry Zorthian, who was chief of the United States Information Agency there and the chief press contact.

"We've had a wire from the White House," Zorthian said, "which says the President wants Reasoner to have every facility."

"You've left out part of it, Barry," I said. "I suspect what it really says is 'We think we've got him bought—don't fuck it up.' "

"That's the next sentence," he said.

I have been talking briefly about Vietnam to make a scene for what is on my mind: my reaction to the first real combat I ever saw. It happened as a result of a long dinner with Ed Fouhy, then CBS News bureau manager in Saigon.

I talked about my previous experience in Vietnam, and I talked about my lack of combat service as either soldier or reporter. What I would like to do, I said, was to take a film crew, take a day or two off from my work on the election documentary, and go to whatever the military thought was the hottest current combat situation. That, said Fouhy, would be somewhere with the Marines, and he would check on it.

He remembered the conversation in the morning and assumed I meant it. There was no practical way to back out.

The Marines said a place called Gio Linh, six miles from the demilitarized zone, was their currently most annoying problem, but they didn't want to take me there. It meant calling attention to the place by sending in a helicopter, probably increasing the already almost constant shelling from across the border, risking a helicopter crew, and giving additional headaches to the Marines stationed there. Fouhy explained I was a senior correspondent with a substantial audience, and he referred them to Barry Zorthian and the White House request. At every stage where I might have been able to get out of the idea gracefully, Fouhy kept pressing, and it was finally agreed I could go up to Gio Linh for the day.

I woke up terrified and stayed terrified. Even as we moved toward Gio Linh, new chances of everything falling apart kept coming up. There was no room, for instance, for me and Kurt Volkert, the cameraman, and a Vietnamese soundman, and my Marine escort officer on the transport planes from Danang to the Marine air base at Phu Bai. At Phu Bai no helicopter had been laid on and nobody wanted to lay one on. My escort officer, apparently giving the impression that I was Lyndon Johnson's illegitimate son and the unacknowledged lover of Marilyn Monroe, got a helicopter.

The helicopter pilot, in the only time he spoke to me all day, laid out the rules. It would be a forty-five-minute flight. When we landed at Gio Linh, we would have five seconds to get out of the helicopter—not an arbitrary time but relating to the observed fact that it usually took the North Vietnamese artillery six seconds to close in and land a shell on some new object at Gio Linh. The pilot was obviously delighted with the chance of spending a non-mission day shepherding a reporter and a cameraman into hostile territory, and not even one of the regular reporters who shared the Marines' life, but an in-and-out visitor, probably a showboater. They would return for us at 1630 hours, he said, and we would have four seconds to get on the helicopter or he would leave us in Gio Linh—probably, his tone implied, forever.

We took off. There were two pilots and an equally unenthusiastic gunner with his feet and gun aimed out the open side hatch. The four of us were strapped in behind the gunner. The countryside looked peaceful enough—there weren't the signs of long years of bombing, the craters that make the countryside nearer Saigon look like one huge erratic golf course and make you wonder if the Air Force ever hit *anything*. We passed over Chu Lai, the northernmost main Marine base, from where truck convoys occasionally resupplied Gio Linh with men and supplies. And then we made a straight-in approach to Gio Linh itself. It looked from the air like a large and littered football field on which the grass had failed, a big red rectangular gouge in a slight elevation, with apparently random arrangements of sandbagged buildings. The landing spot was just outside the perimeter, and we hit it without ceremony, and the four visitors got out well within the five-second deadline. The helicopter rose immediately, and we crouched under its wind and ran toward a sort of gate. There awaited us one of the angriest men I have ever met, a major, the camp commander, a career Marine. No one had told him we were coming; he was of the opinion that any helicopter visit stirred up his opponents up the road, which would mean that for the day he would have an extra two or three casualties and maybe a couple of deaths; he didn't like reporters anyway, and he particularly didn't like television crews, and, on first sight, he felt especially strongly that he didn't like us. My escort officer started to explain, and I said mildly, "As long as we're here..."

As long as we were there, he indicated, the first thing would be to get under cover before some reporter, or maybe even someone valuable, got killed. We started toward his command shack. At the northwest end of the rectangle there was an old open tower, a relic of the days when this was a French outpost, and on top of it was a Marine with glasses. Suddenly he yelled, "Incoming!" and the reason for the lacework of trenches I had noticed became evident. I was shoved abruptly into one by the red-haired, red-faced major. A second later there was an explosion. "You see what I mean," he said with relative calm. "That's the first incoming of the day, and it's because you stirred them up."

I didn't mark the occasion at the moment—I was too

scared—but it was an occasion: for the first time in my life I had been fired at in anger—not me personally fired at or with personal anger at me, but it counted, I think. It is an extremely absorbing feeling.

There were two more shouts of "Incoming!" and two more dives into trenches before we reached the command bunker, and three much louder explosions, our artillery replying in the desultory game we had apparently initiated. The shells that were coming in were howitzer shells, shrapnel; you were relatively safe in a trench from anything but a direct hit, but the area within twenty yards or so of where the shell landed was highly dangerous, sprayed with whistling, hot, sharp shards of metal. You usually had two or three seconds from the warning cry to find a trench, and it was usually plenty of time; you tend to move fairly fast in the circumstances. Once I landed on Volkert's back, grinding him and his camera into the red dirt. I apologized.

In the bunker the major became more friendly: he was stuck with us for the day, and I suppose the natural feeling was to enjoy seeing a strange face. I liked him, and—I suppose because of the shells that were aimed at me as well as at him, the Marines, and the American way of life—I had a strong, immediate sympathy for him and the problems of his command.

Gio Linh, like so many things in that damned war, was of no practical use. It was too exposed to be used as a base for patrols: a patrol leaving its perimeter was an immediate open target. The patrols were run from Chu Lai to the south. Gio Linh was there only to prove that it could be there: it was the presence of the United States of America. It was a particularly heart-breaking assignment for a commander because there was no way to take any affirmative action against the enemy; you couldn't get out at him, you had to just sit there and know that over any thirty-day period— Marines went up there on thirty-day tours—you would lose a half-dozen dead and twenty or so wounded. And there was no way of knowing if your return fire did any damage, or whether the concussions at night from B-52's bombing a couple of miles to the north meant that they were hitting anything. It was, for the Marines there, a kind of Russian roulette in which you didn't even have the thrill of spinning the chamber yourself.

He said we could walk around the base and make pictures and talk to anybody we wanted to. He was particularly proud of a bank of showerheads he had rigged: in that muggy heat and dirt, unrestricted showers were a bigger morale aid than movies. We made the tour. It took quite a while because of the continuing shelling and the diving into the trenches. I felt frustrated because there was no safe way to see a shell land and explode; flat in the shallow trench, you heard the noise and the whistling of the released metal, but we had no pictures to take home. I suggested to Kurt that when the next shell came he crouch above the trench and record its landing; I, I explained, could be describing what went on from the trench. He declined for some reason, probably not the reason he gave, which was that it would be cinematically more effective if *he* was in the trench, photographing me against the sky as I watched the landing shell.

While we were there, in spite of the fairly heavy activity,

there was only one casualty, a man taking one of those cold showers. Maybe he had soap in his ears and didn't hear the warning, maybe he figured the hell with it. I never did find out if he died.

We were crouched against the sandbagged perimeter in plenty of time for the helicopter's return; we didn't move out to the pad until we heard it and saw it, because there were no trenches there. It was the same silent crew; we got on board well within our four-second allotment and whirled away from beautiful Gio Linh. I felt, for the first time, a feeling that is common among combat reporters, I think: a regret, almost a shame, at leaving the soldiers. In a war, particularly a war like Vietnam, the regular reporters and cameramen probably see more danger than the soldiers and Marines; certainly in Vietnam their casualty rate was higher than that of any of the services. But there are these occasions: *you* head for Danang and a steak at the officers' club or Saigon and the air-conditioned Caravelle; *they* stay there and read paperback books in the smell and dirt of the bunkers. You feel for the poor sons-of-bitches. But you leave.

At Phu Bai I got lucky: a quick ride in one of the transports to Danang and an almost immediate connection to Saigon on the civilian airline, Air Vietnam. I would, I realized, be back in Saigon in time for a late dinner if Air Vietnam's DC-4 stayed up in the air. It turned out there was some question of that. We approached Tan Son Nhut across Cho Lon in heavy thunder shower; there was a time when the plane, quite apparently in trouble, lumbered up and away from the river and made a long circle to try again. So I stayed terrified. But we landed, and there was a CBS driver to meet me, and by nine o'clock I was back in the Caravelle, sitting in my icy room with a drink. Jack Laurence, the young man who was one of the best war correspondents for television, came in and said some nice things about senior correspondents who didn't have to go to places like Gio Linh going there. I thanked him modestly and said it was nothing.

But of course it *was* something for me, and in the five minutes after he left, it came to me, in one of those great realizations you get about life—one of those great realizations that hold up for future examination, I mean, not the other kind.

It had been, as noted, a day of terror, the kind of gripping of all your internal organs that I had read enough about in war books but had never known, hours of trying not to show to your fellows how terrified you are, of trying to do your job while the terror goes on. It wasn't that you had to be ashamed of being scared; they all get scared—the reporters like Bert Quint who have spent most of their lives being shot at, it must seem; the career Marines; the draftees. People who don't have enough sense to get scared don't make good soldiers—or good reporters. But people who when they get scared get immobilized don't make very good ones either.

So—I had gotten through it, creditably. For all I knew, I might never hear another shot in my life. (I was wrong.) I was back in a reasonably secure hotel and had a pleasant dinner ahead of me. Then why did I feel a deep and somber letdown that in a way was worse than the griping and breath-shortening fright of the long day?

The answer, I think, is part of what explains wars. Because the terror had been so completely absorbing, the feeling of being alive after peril had occurred so often during that day, the preoccupation with the situation of hazard had been so entire, all awareness of other, real, insoluble problems of life had been wiped out, and now oozed back into what should have been the relieved and smug consciousness.

When you are playing war, nothing else matters, and if you can live through the next five minutes, you can live forever. But when you do live through it, and go home or to a reasonable substitute, everything else comes back. Now life is suddenly flat and tasteless because again you have to worry about lung cancer and romance and employment and alcohol and money—all the things which are *not* solved by the simple matter of where the next shell lands or the next bullet is aimed. You are back in the real world, and everyone knows what a mess that is.

It explains why people become career soldiers, war-lovers, and mercenaries. But it also explains why, for so long in history, ordinary people have been willing to go. The fact is, for millions of Americans, World War II *did* encompass the Best Years of Their Lives.

If Vietnam did a service, it was to put that feeling of excitement into balance; I think it will make other wars, for civilized countries, harder.

But I lay there in the Caravelle and realized that, given a choice between going ahead and interviewing President Thieu the next day, as I was scheduled to do, or going to some other battle scene in a helicopter, I might very well choose the fight, terrorized instantly after the decision, but absorbed. Nothing is so completely absorbing as combat except unusually rewarding and intimate passion, and I suppose, through the centuries, for most people, combat has been easier to find.

11

60 Minutes

IF A DEDICATION of a book of this kind should express
awareness of the people who made the career it describes
possible, it's easy to think of a half-dozen people who would
be perfectly suitable—Dick Salant, for instance, or Sig
Mickelson, or Mitch Charnley, or Jim Bormann. Or the two
women most prominent in my personal life, who helped
with a combination of goading and cheering and patience.
Or Bill Small, who brought me back to CBS, or, or, or . . .
The people who have helped me even at times when
probably what they *wanted* to do was hit me sharply over
the head would make quite a list.

As you may have noticed, I chose to dedicate the book
to Don Hewitt, on the grounds that if I had to pick a man
who has had more than anyone else to do with what I got a
chance to do and how I did it, it would be Don.

This doesn't mean that Don and I are great friends.

There was a time in 1963 or early 1964, for instance, when Don quite seriously and formally asked Dick Salant to arrange it so that he would never have to work with me again. I forget what I had done: probably something innocuous. Don says he doesn't remember what it was either.

We are certainly not drinking buddies who sit around and talk about life and the profession and the nature of our dedication. I don't think Don does that much with anybody; certainly not with me. But from the very early days I think he saw that I could help him do the things he wanted to do, and gave me the chance. The culmination of that process, of course, was a little program called *60 Minutes,* which Don asked me to help him start in 1968.

In the spring of 1968 I don't think either Don or I was in terribly great shape professionally. He was rather in the position of Winston Churchill in 1946 when, as he put it, after he had successfully led the preservation of the British Empire in its darkest hour, the British voters rewarded him by turning him out of office. Don and Walter Cronkite had made the *CBS Evening News* the model of its kind; Fred Friendly rewarded Don by relieving him of the executive producership of the evening news. I don't know why. If I had to guess, I would guess Fred felt about Don much as he felt about me: smart guy, maybe brilliant, but not *sérieux.*

So Don had some things to do—specials and conventions and things like that—but no real outlet for his energies. Then, with Salant back in the news presidency after Fred's departure, he talked Salant into letting him make an inexpensive pilot for a weekly news magazine of the air. It was a new if not revolutionary idea. What was different about it was that it would be neither portentous documentary nor a news of the week in review.

The initial idea was that it would be a compendium of two or three or four pieces in an hour by a number of correspondents, but that, for the pilot at least, there would be a host—a correspondent who might do some of the stories himself. Don asked me if I would stay in one night when he had gotten some allotted studio time and host the pilot. I said sure, I owed him a wasted evening—but I also said it was a hopeless project. Because, I said, it inevitably, like *Who, What, When, Where, Why,* involved singling out one correspondent, and CBS News management, remembering being prisoners of Murrow and already against their will becoming something like prisoners of Cronkite—CBS management would never stand for that.

I felt that I was doing the man a favor.

We put together some re-cut segments from shows that had already been on the air—one, I remember, was a piece Kuralt had done on Henry Ford—and produced the pilot, and executives looked at it. In the next few weeks, in sessions to which I was not privy and in the processes that go on in Don Hewitt's mind when he walks down halls, several decisions were made. One was that along with me the broadcast needed a very different personality. The most different personality from me in all of CBS News was Mike Wallace, and he and I made a second pilot.

The second decision was Don's, and—I won't be sure until he reads this and tells me, and maybe not even then—the second decision was that the hosts in general would also be the *only* reporters. What I am not sure of is whether or not this was a conscious decision. In any event, the program went on the air in the fall of 1968, every other Tuesday sometimes, to what is referred to as critical acclaim. It didn't do all that badly, considering that it was on opposite the then most popular show on television—*Marcus Welby, M.D.*—but it looked as if it would fall into that familiar category of good-intentioned and well-done news programs that last awhile and then fade.

Except that Hewitt stuck with it, and Wallace stuck with it, and CBS stuck with it. And that for producers and correspondents and camera crews it was the most satisfying and delightful thing they had ever done.

I didn't stick with it, of course; after a couple of months of our third season I went to ABC News. But by then it had established a personality and a loyal audience in and out of CBS. I have to report in honesty that when I left, *60 Minutes* was something like the fiftieth most popular program in television. When I returned, to become the fourth correspondent (Morley Safer had replaced me and a couple of years later they had added Dan Rather), it was practically always among the ten most popular programs. Actually, the week before I went back on the air on *60 Minutes*, Don came in on a Wednesday morning and said, "You can go back to ABC, we were number one last week." But I also have to say defensively that for the first full season that I was back, the broadcast was for the first time—and for the incredible first time for any news broadcast—the most popular American television program of the year. Mike Wallace says that is a coincidence, but he is touchy.

Why? What is it about *60 Minutes*? Well, one thing goes back to the second, perhaps unconscious decision of the early months—that there would be not hosts but reporters. Don says now that what you have is a situation in which Mike and Morley and Dan and Harry are the only Richard Harding Davises left in the news world. Everybody—print and broadcasting—has bureaus now, and they do the hard news. Only Mike and Morley and Dan and Harry go everywhere, from Hoboken to Libya, from Palm Springs to Rapid City. We are reporters. We obviously couldn't do it if the five producers assigned to each correspondent did not also go everywhere, at considerably more length and with more involvement in each story. But each of the correspondents spends enough of himself on each story to qualify as a reporter, and I think people sense that.

What else? Hewitt and the producers, especially senior producer Palmer Williams. Hewitt, as you may have sensed in other parts of this account, is an authentic genius of television news. Williams is the man who filters Hewitt's genius and makes it work. (He is phasing himself out in favor of my old assignment-desk colleague Phil Scheffler, who may well turn out to have the same peculiar talent.) But Hewitt—when I came back after eight years, it is a measure of how well I knew him that I was not surprised to find that after more than twenty-five years in the business he still had the same boundless enthusiasm for every story, the same instinctive touch with how to do it, the same impatience with being bored or boring anyone.

What else? Well, what in retrospect seems to have been

the faith of CBS News in the broadcast, the decision to put it on at seven o'clock eastern time on Sunday and leave it there and not pre-empt it or cut it short for a football game.

But this is supposed to be about the early years, when Mike and I and Don and Palmer were figuring out how to do it, while I worked at it only part of the time. It sort of got itself together and grew and got a personality. And it was always fun. Early on—and I don't remember whose idea it was—we developed a concept that worked very well when there were only two correspondents: Mike would take one side of a story and I would take the other. This led to a strange but I think acceptable journalistic tactic: we could become somewhat less objective, we were briefly advocates, knowing that the other side would have its advocate, too. It worked. It worked in the very early months of Northern Ireland's long agony, where I reported the Catholic side and Mike the Protestant; it worked twice in the Middle East, where first Mike took the Israelis and I took the Arabs and then, a few months later, we reversed our roles. It worked beautifully in the Biafran civil war, where Mike went to Lagos and got dysentery and Jeff Gralnick and Keith Kay and I went to the Biafran side of the war zone and got shot at. I should note that this was not a case of Mike choosing the cushy side of the story; we flipped a coin. His coin, as I remember it.

So it was great to come back to, except I had forgotten how hard it is, and I got into some trouble. It *is* hard. It is somewhere between 120 and 140 days of travel every year. It is, if you count the July doldrums and the Jewish holidays and the hiatus at Thanksgiving and Christmas, the necessity for a correspondent to complete a story a week and for producers to average a story every five weeks. It is true that Dan Rather, calling in to ask his assistant about some arrangements, was asked where he was calling from. He had to open the phone-booth door and inquire of an airport passer-by. "Atlanta," he said. And it's true that once when I was playing catch-up on several stories in several locations, on a morning at the end I woke in a panic and poked the person next to me. "My God," I said, "did we leave a call?" "You're home, stupid," she said.

So it is the best job in journalism, and it wouldn't be if it were not fun. From the moment the program began to be important, Fred Friendly had an ambivalent attitude toward it: he was quite seriously delighted that a news broadcast could attract a mass audience, but he didn't think, with an opportunity like that to reach people, that *60 Minutes* was serious enough.

Fred Friendly doesn't think anyone is serious enough.

The return to *60 Minutes* makes a good place, I think, to talk a little about how things have changed—about whether or not, as I mentioned early on, this craft has grown and where it's going. Well, it has certainly grown in a physical way: the number of people employed by CBS News has increased at a far faster rate than the amount of air time filled by CBS News. My first assignment when I returned to *60 Minutes* was with Walter Dombrow, one of the great cameraman when you get his attention, and we talked about the differences since we first worked together—he and I and a soundman then, arriving at a story cold, being producers and writers and correspondents and photographers all at once. And now—a first-class field producer (Drew Phillips in this case, as first-class as you can get) a week ahead of us on the story, a minimum four-man crew, an attention to quality and depth we never had the time for. But we agreed that, at least in a case where the group was Phillips and Dombrow and me, the process hadn't changed that much. We used the huge influence of *60 Minutes*, the extra time involved on the scene, the great editors back in the office, the knowledge that we had to make this clear and interesting to Hewitt and Scheffler and Williams. All of these things combined to make our work better—not different. We still had to know how to get it and how to write it and make a picture of it. So that part is all right; we haven't gotten soft. Dombrow has been doing this kind of thing even a little longer than I have—and I think he follows the same rule Don Hewitt does. He can stand getting tired, but the day it gets boring he quits.

A digression: Walter likes to play when the workday is done, even if it interferes with his sleep (I don't know *when* he sleeps). I should make it clear that by play I mean something innocent, because I have frequently joined him. In early 1980 we were doing a story in a small Ohio city, and before I even got there the crew had developed the habit of stopping after work for a beer and dinner at a pleasant downtown bar. Walter had been using his son Mark as an assistant cameraman, and he was there, of course. The day I arrived we did some filming at the bar—

something about what the man on the street, or in this case the men and women at the bar, thought about the story. After we were done, we filled up a couple of tables and it turned into a sort of party. For reasons not quite clear even at the time, it seemed like a good idea to Walter to introduce Mark as *my* son. (Incidentally, Mark said later he did a great deal better as my son than as Walter's.) People took this as interesting but not sensational. Then I left—through the years I have frequently left early, thank God—and a woman who had been at the bar with the crew for several evenings told Walter she was puzzled.

"I don't understand," she said. "Last night you introduced Mark as your son, and now you say he's Harry's. Which is he?"

"Well, I'll tell you," said Walter. "Harry and I have worked together very closely for twenty-five years. We never really knew."

The woman, under the Dombrow spell, found that an acceptable answer; she couldn't know that I have never met Walter Dombrow's wife of some thirty years. Walter likes to sow harmless confusion.

As in another case: I arrived late at night at a rendezvous motel; producer and crew had gone to bed, except for Walter, chatting with a local lady at the bar. It developed that she felt a claim to fame: in her salad days she had had a long affair with a man who went on to become one of the most popular news broadcasters in the East.

"I know him very well," Walter said. "Did you know he finally came out of the closet about his homosexuality?"

The woman was, as we used to say, thunder and struck. "I can't believe it," she said, "I just can't believe it. . . . Why, for three years we . . ."

"I know," Walter said sympathetically. "Everyone was surprised."

Walter Dombrow. Unique, probably fortunately, and an authentic genius at lighting and composing and taking pictures. I'll give you one clue, if you ever meet him: when he starts beginning sentences with "Seriously, though," watch out.

THE MENTION of the four-man crews—cameraman, assistant, soundman, and electrician—brings up a couple of other observations. When you add a producer and a correspondent and sometimes a researcher and descend on a story with thirty or forty cases of equipment, people sometimes feel a little overwhelmed. But we really work very economically. For the British Broadcasting Corporation to make the kind of story that we get for *60 Minutes*, union rules would require eleven people in the crew. And our union crews work hard. They are, I believe, well paid. I don't know anyone who comes closer to earning his money.

And a technical note that leads into something else: at this writing, *60 Minutes* is the only major network news enterprise that still uses, chiefly, film film as opposed to videotape cameras. We do it because you can get a picture— a defined picture with the shadows and contrasts and emphasis of life itself—with careful use of film and light that you cannot yet get with tape. Tape shows everything within range, but it also gives everything an equal value. Film is like a writer recording a scene with an illumination in his head; tape is like an inventory of the scene, untouched by human hands. We'll be forced into tape sooner or later; it is for a lot of reasons the wave of the future. The hope is that the Dombrows of the next generation will find a way to tame and mold it for quality journalism, for, as is our task, highlighting and explaining life. I expect they will.

Anyway, the problem is not how you take pictures. It's what you take pictures of, and what you say about them. I spoke very early in this book about my professional life encompassing the infancy of this monster, its precocious and generally beloved childhood, its troubled and besieged youth, and what is perhaps its premature old age. That's what worries me, frankly. The youth was the novelty. It was John Cameron Swayze and a newsreel-style evening news report (I wasn't watching at the time, but I'm told authoritatively that his NBC broadcast had a regular feature which he introduced by saying, "And now, hopscotching the world by dateline") being replaced by Huntley and Brinkley and the first television news report with style. It was Hewitt making the Edwards show the first real attempt to let *reporters*, some with pencils and some with cameras, *report* the news and take a reporter's responsibility for doing it. It was giving Americans the objective evidence for making up their own minds about Little Rock or Cyprus or John Kennedy versus Richard Nixon. That was the childhood, I think, and the time the monster became beloved.

Then the youth—when television news began to show not only solvable problems, like Little Rock, but seemingly insoluble things like assassination and hatred and alienation and a morass called Vietnam. There was an almost irresistible temptation for Americans to conclude that the thing that showed you all this was a major cause of all this. There was an almost irresistible dual impulse in the craft. The dual impulse: on the part of the working younger people, to become advocates and pitch things a great deal stronger; on the part of the establishment within our craft, to ease off a little. It was, for America, a time of unprecedented national introspection following the Kennedy assassination, a time when we began questioning all kinds of unquestioned national values, a time when our most thoughtful conservatives were disgusted and the best and brightest of our youth was alienated and rudderless. It was the time that produced Spiro Agnew (you remember Spiro Agnew) voicing the inchoate feeling of a lot of people that somehow those of us whose job was to tell you what was going on were creating what was going on.

We got through that, and I think for two reasons. One was that Mr. Agnew's charges and the sad feelings of so many citizens were inaccurate: we were not creating the malaise, we were reporting it. The second reason is that because of the tradition that William Paley and Edward R. Murrow began, and maybe most of all because of Walter Cronkite, people didn't believe Agnew or the snake of suspicion in their own minds. I remember flying from Denver to Rapid City in the summer of 1972 to interview the newly selected Democratic nominee, Senator McGovern. The pilot announced that Spiro Agnew had been on board the week before, and that I was on board that day. The response to me, I thought, was much warmer than to the name of Agnew. What did it prove? That, as Cronkite had never questioned and I had never questioned, it was our country as well as Mr. Nixon's and Agnew's; that we were as proud and conscious of being Americans as any of the guys with flags in their lapels; that in this country you don't solve problems by concealing them. You don't solve them by pouring gasoline on them and setting them afire either, and I'm not saying journalism is guiltless. I'm saying we are all on the same side, and the people in the airplane knew that; it was Mr. Agnew who missed the point.

No, we got through that troubled youth. It's just that now—except for *60 Minutes* and a few other things, the fun seems to have gone out of it. (Fred Friendly will love that.) On account of having a lot of children who kept getting younger as I kept getting older, I have had the chastening experience (actually, it was the children's mother who first commented on this) of being the oldest person at a PTA meeting. I sometimes have the same baffled feeling as I look at the young reporters. They are so damned competitive and ethnically and sexually balanced and so delighted with the new toys that enable them to be on the air first with some story no one should be expected to care about. I blame the colleges, partly: so many of them took broadcast journalism out of journalism and put it in something called a "Communications" major, turning out people who knew all about how but not what to communicate.

And I blame a fortuity: the increasing profitability of news. When the news department was a bleeding drain of money you kept going to stay out of trouble with the FCC;

the scruffy types in the newsroom could experiment and fool around, with the dollar the only stricture. Now they are studied and courted and analyzed. And they move around like vaudevillians moving up the old circuits. It produces situations like one I ran into a year or so ago doing some promotional work for a West Virginia station. The station's anchor staff was there. It turned out I knew more about Charleston than they did; they were on their way somewhere, building a résumé to move on to Cleveland or Chicago or maybe even Los Angeles or New York. They were nice enough kids, but Charleston—or Des Moines or Miami— deserves something else, and this is management's problem. Don't put too much hair spray on the goose that has begun to tentatively lay golden eggs. Geese with too much hair spray sink.

THIS SECTION STARTED OUT to be about *60 Minutes* and wandered. I'd like to go back a moment to suggest another reason why *60 Minutes* has done so well. It is the instinctive premise that all of reality is the grist of news. In anthropology you are as interested in cooking pots and games as in thrones and religions; so is *60 Minutes*. So we erratically touch on art and trivia and pool hustlers and old ladies who own Rolls-Royces as well as on rip-offs and shahs and chancellors. This is, given the world we live in, as it should be.

12

Coming Apart

O<small>N ELECTION NIGHT IN</small> 1964 I worked at a desk with Roger Mudd. Our assignment was to keep track of the presidential race. It became clear very early that it was not a very complicated job, that Lyndon Johnson was going to win by the century's fourth landslide and that such interest in the broadcast as existed was in the analysis of why—which occupied Eric Sevareid and Walter Cronkite more than it did Roger and me—and in the stories of other races.

I had not at that point, of course, heard a remark made by Howard K. Smith as he and I wound up, for ABC, the co-anchoring of the election-night broadcast in 1972 and it had become obvious that Richard Nixon was defeating George McGovern in the century's *fifth* landslide. Remember that in November 1972 Mr. Nixon was riding very high indeed. There seemed to be some progress toward an end of the American bleeding in Indochina; he had brought realism back to our relations with China; the economy was not yet blatantly displaying the inner wounds that the years in Vietnam had caused. If it weren't for the persistent distrust that many people still had of Mr. Nixon—justifiably, of course, as it turned out—the atmosphere at the end of election night was almost like the apparent national harmony that heralded James Monroe's Era of Good Feeling, and I may have made some idiotic remark to that effect. Howard, with the perception and intuition that have always set him apart in journalism, had some reservations—and remember, at that point he would have been seen as a supporter of many of Richard Nixon's policies.

"I don't know, Harry," he said. "I can't help but recall that every landslide victory in this century has been followed by disaster for the President who won it—if you define a landslide as sixty percent of the popular vote. Harding did it and we had Teapot Dome and criminal trials for his close associates. Hoover did it in 1928. Roosevelt did it in 1936 and immediately plunged into the scheme to pack the Supreme Court that tarnished a part of his image forever. Johnson did it in 1964 and you know what happened after that."

I think I chuckled; there were not many prescient enough that night to foresee disaster for Richard Nixon.

Anyhow, in the 1964 landslide I think my superiors were pleased enough with what Roger and I did with what we had. Two years later, in the off-year election in 1966, I was assigned to report on the races for the House of Representatives. And in 1968 I had no election assignment at all.

If you are wondering where this catalog is going, this is where it is going: it was because of the non-assignment in 1968 that I was psychologically ready to leave CBS two years later when my contract expired. What had happened was that in 1966 Bill Leonard had been extremely dissatisfied with my performance. Everything that happened that night, in his view, confirmed all the things he thought about me, the diagnosis that had been begun almost carelessly by Fred Friendly that I was talented but lazy, a fine man on the air but apt to be unprepared, a good writer but a less-than-*sérieux* reporter. (I keep using the French word because I used it once with Friendly and I don't think he knew what it meant; I'm sure Leonard does and would also know it means something a little different from "serious.") I don't know whether he was right or not; I had thought I did pretty well in 1966, but some people whose judgment I respect agreed with Leonard when he told them. So I can't be sure. What I can be sure of was that it was hard to understand that Leonard said absolutely nothing to me.

I found out in this way: in the late summer of 1968, when other people began to get the research material and paperwork in preparation for election night, I didn't get any. I finally went to Bob Chandler, who was directing the operation under Leonard, and he told me—painedly, I think; I think he thought, too, I ought to have been told before—essentially what I outlined above. I went on to see Leonard, who confirmed the same essentials.

It was not what you would call a good winter. I remember thinking of a line in *Brideshead Revisited* by Evelyn

Waugh. An army officer stands, after the war, looking over the deserted site of a camp where he had come to grips with war and armies and commanders, and the line is: "Here love had died between me and the army." In my case it was in Bill Leonard's office, and love died between me and the hierarchy of CBS News. It was, as it turned out, rekindleable, but at the time it was, except for the giving up of the love of a woman, the most wrenching experience I had ever had.

I thought back to moments of devotion and triumph— to the only interview with Lyndon Johnson anyone had been able to get for CBS at Atlantic City in 1964, to the long night charters and the desperate drives to Little Rock and Montgomery and Nashville, to the landing shells at Gio Linh, to *Calendar* and *CBS Reports* and the fourteen-hour marathon when the Pope came to New York, to the triumph nights of the Sunday news and the long summer substitutions for Cronkite, to all of the feelings I had had about CBS News all my life. There is an old word for what I was: I was heartsick.

I suppose if you dreamed all your life of being a naval officer or an infantry commander or a fighter pilot, and made it, and were praised, and felt a good deal of the time that slight thickening in the throat, that mild feeling that a great athlete must have that you know exactly what you are doing and how to do it, that almost goatish interior calmness which says to the people you are working with, "Don't worry, I have it"—I suppose if your life has been like that and then you are finally told forget it, you have a future as a laundry and morale officer or a kick-off return specialist or second officer on a transport plane—I suppose it would feel like that. What Mr. Leonard in effect said to me was that I was highly valuable to CBS News in certain ways, but that I could not pull my weight in certain heavy areas. There were three ways to react to that. I couldn't hit him because you don't do that at CBS. As Adlai Stevenson said after he lost in 1952, I was too big to cry and it hurt too much to laugh. That left the third alternative: go somewhere where I would be appreciated, somewhere where Cronkite and Sevareid and Kuralt and all those people didn't cut holes in my penumbra—somewhere where Bill Leonard wasn't.

Since my return to CBS, Bill Leonard has, I must admit, been more than fair. We talked about my resentments and agreed to start over, and I have no complaints. I'm sorry, Bill, for whatever part of it is my fault.

Anyhow, what it came down to in the fall of 1970 is that I was heartsick. And what it led to was ABC News.

My contract expired in November 1970, and for some months before that my agent had tried to negotiate a new one. In each meeting the CBS attitude was the same: after seven years they were unprepared to offer me one dollar more in a new agreement. I think I can be excused for feeling that this was a *New Yorker* magazine "Words of One Syllable" item. They had at the time a richness of experienced and popular correspondents; they stood well ahead of NBC, and ABC News was not yet a full competitor. So when we told them that we were serious, and that unless some kind of offer was made we would look elsewhere, I don't think they believed it—or in paranoid moments I thought their decision was to regretfully let me go, saving

$100,000 a year or so in the news budget and coasting along with Cronkite and Sevareid and Kuralt and Wallace.

This was, of course, the time when a kind gesture, a pat on the head, a lunch at "21" would have changed things. I didn't know anything but CBS News and didn't want to; *60 Minutes* was beginning to form itself into the massive delight it got to be later; I was Walter Cronkite about twenty percent of the year. But there was no gesture. Dick Salant said nobody ever told him what was going on; Bill Leonard was busy encouraging me to prove myself as a reporter by working on the radio desk election night.

There was another element that is hard to realize now, but I was the Curt Flood, or more properly the Andy Messersmith, of broadcast news: no senior correspondent before had ever gone amicably from one network to another as a free agent, simply for a better job and more money. As Ernest Hemingway said about Lady Brett Ashley's hair style, she started all that.

I don't think you want any great detail about why another network wanted me (there is a thing in television called a "Q" rating, which is sort of a statistic relating the number of people who recognize you to the number of people who feel favorable about you; I have a very high "Q" rating, which may indicate that a lot of people in this country are no more *sérieux* than I am), or about why I wanted to go (I wanted to be an anchorman once before I died and the only tiger in the zoo). And so far as how things went, they went very well for a while and then ABC and I, in one of the major achievements of modern journalism, combined to blow the whole thing.

Coming Apart

· · ·

ON THE FIRST MONDAY of November 1970 I met in a room of the Dorset Hotel in New York with my agent, the ineffable Ralph Mann, and a sort of delegation from ABC News.

On that morning things had proceeded to a point of Decision. Ralph had had innumerable conversations with ABC, and most things had been satisfactorily agreed upon— money, length of contract, all the things that can cause you trouble if you don't get them clearly in writing. That's why you have agents and companies have business lawyers.

Which makes me inclined to a digression. I have nowhere else in this book talked about my agents, and if you don't mind, I'd like to. My agents are Marvin Josephson and Ralph Mann, and at this writing they are respectively chairman and vice chairman of a huge operation called International Creative Management, Inc. I say "at this writing," because in my twenty years with Marvin and Ralph the corporate name has changed a half-dozen times. Marvin kept deciding he didn't like the agency business and that he was going to cut down to just a few news-type clients, and he would do that and I would suddenly be represented by something called Broadcast Management instead of Marvin Josephson Associates. It has never made any difference. Except for the incredibly smart woman in the literary department of the agency who led me gently into this book, I have never dealt with anyone at the firm, whatever it was called at the moment, except Marvin and Ralph. I love them both. They have saved my life and sanity on a number of occasions.

If you are aware of agents, as we all are from reading

esoteric material like *People* magazine and Harold Robbins, a couple of questions occur to you. First, why does a simple news correspondent need an agent, and, second, why does a simple news correspondent—whose income, and thence the agency's commission, at even the highest level pales in comparison to movie stars and rock groups and unclassifiable people like Wayne Newton—why does a simple news correspondent get represented by the chairman and vice chairman of an organization which has dozens—maybe hundreds, for all I know—of agents negotiating for all kinds of people who bring in a lot more money than any reporter, and who may never meet Ralph and Marvin?

Two questions, two answers: once you get beyond the journeyman level in broadcast journalism, you need an agent because you need someone who is as concerned about your welfare as you are, as nervous and anxious for your success and acclaim as you are, who is, in short, as egotistic about you as you are—but who doesn't get his feelings hurt. This is a key to a professional relationship with your superiors. You and they are talking about the proper way to cover a story in the same way a regular reporter would talk to his city editor; somewhere down the hall your agent is arguing with the company's business-affairs representative about whether you deserve a raise; a good agent will tell you when you don't and get it for you when you do.

Second answer: I don't know about other agents and agencies, but I think for Marvin and Ralph their news clients are their hobbies, their relaxation when they need relief from the tension of big deals and temperaments and things which can go one way or the other and make or lose a

hundred million dollars. At current salary levels, we pay our
way, of course. But most of it we pay in something else than
money. This just my theory. Ask Marvin. Ask Ralph. On
second thought, don't ask Ralph. He will worry about it and
bawl me out at lunch.

I was talking the other day to Dave Klinger, who was
director of business affairs at CBS in my first tour there. I
signed my first one-year contract without reading it; I was
on such a natural high at being named a correspondent I
would have signed papers voluntarily accepting serfhood.
(Actually, that's not far from what the first contract specified.) Then came time for the second contract, and Dave and
I were recalling, twenty-one years later, that our big argument, the argument that almost resulted in my leaving CBS
in 1959 instead of 1970, was over $25 a week. I said it was a
simple Iowa matter of being able to put meat on my family's
table, and Dave was fair and finally said okay. (Other, less
perceptive and skilled negotiators at other networks have
lost good people over $25 a week.) But it was an exhausting
experience, and humbling.

Then, in the week before the Jack Gould column that
turned my career around, Marvin Josephson invited me to
lunch. I knew who he was—a former CBS attorney who had
started an agency (I forget what he first called it) and was
specializing in news people. We went to the Oak Room at
the Plaza Hotel; I had never been there.

Marvin said that he would like to represent me. I did
something like a chuckle. In a good week, I pointed out to
him, I made something like $275, and to take $27.50 out of
that would seriously affect my standard of living and not

materially enrich his young company. I said that Kuralt, not me, was the rising star at CBS and I was depressed and stagnant.

He said he would propose two things—first, since my income was low and he was investing in a future, he would exempt $200 a week from his ten-percent commission for as long as I wanted, and, second, that he and I would agree that, no matter what we signed or for how long, it would always be cancelable by either party on twenty-four hours' notice. When things changed abruptly in the next few weeks and my income went up like a lovely balloon, I joyously asked that the $200 exemption be dropped. In twenty years we have never changed the second provision, and never wanted to—at least I haven't.

There is a further digression here. Every time I have ever signed a contract, along with the pleasure at new income or new challenge, there is an old—sexist, I guess—feeling that somehow I have been seduced. Your freedom of choice, your chastity, in a way, is gone for one or two or seven years. You wonder, in the back of your mind, if the company will respect you in the morning.

ELMER LOWER, then president of ABC News, headed their little group, which included, as I remember it, his vice president, Bill Sheehan, and their business-affairs director, Martin Rubenstein. Elmer, an alumnus of CBS, had kept ABC's standards high and its news budgets growing in spite of a series of failures to achieve anything like a respectable third place in audience ratings. There were a lot of reasons for this—the third network to get started would in any event have taken a long time to win the acceptance that CBS News had. One of the nice things about news when you are on top is that people's news-watching habits change slowly. One of the bad things when you are on the bottom is that same fact.

There were really only two things to decide that day: would I accept the job of co-anchor of the *ABC Evening News*, and if I did, would it be the *ABC Evening News with Harry Reasoner and Howard K. Smith* or the *ABC Evening News with Howard K. Smith and Harry Reasoner*? I agreed without much fuss—because it was obviously the proper thing to do—to take second place in the title. But I had some reservations about saying yes—partly the previously noted feeling that, no matter how good the money or how high the purpose, nice girls don't say yes; partly a more realistic question about ABC's commitment to trying to be a real competitor in the news business. A survey had shown ABC that if they couldn't get Walter Cronkite, I was the next most popular man with American news audiences. But that's not enough. A man audiences like and trust can help a good news organization raise its ratings, but he can't help a bad organization. Elmer Lower thought he knew how to deal with that concern, and he was right. He and everyone else left the room, and Elton Rule, the president of American Broadcasting Companies, came in to talk to me. He told me ABC's commitment was sincere and strong. He said things I believed in—and CBS had always believed in—like "I think, whether it's profitable or not, news has a lap-over effect: a respected and aggressive news department increases your general audience in a way that's hard to measure." I liked him and I believed him and I was obviously flattered at being courted by the man second only to chairman Leonard Goldenson at ABC. I said I would take the job, and everyone else came back in the room and we all had Bloody Marys.

Elton Rule is a big, handsome man who could have succeeded Frank Stanton as the statesman of the broadcast industry, except that he didn't really want to. He hated to make speeches or lobby in Washington. For an incredibly ebullient and successful salesman, he was in other ways strangely shy. But he was that day and through all the years straight and level with me. What went wrong wasn't his fault, except maybe for some inattention.

So we had an agreement, and the decision was to announce it on the following Thursday. I don't know how a group as experienced in broadcast business as this one was could be so naïve as to think the secret could be kept three days, but I wanted time to tell CBS, and Elmer Lower wanted time to tell Frank Reynolds, who had been co-anchor with Smith.

A note about that: I was taking Reynolds' job, and you feel bad about that, but that's the way it is. You don't cheat to get a job, but if you get it, you don't feel guilty—or at least you try not to. And things tend to even out. I don't know anyone at a senior level who has not lost some; even Walter Cronkite was capriciously replaced as convention anchor after CBS did badly at the Republican convention in 1964. And things can even out dramatically. I took Frank Reynolds' job in 1970; when I left ABC under something less than ideal circumstances in 1978, who replaced me as senior anchor? Frank Reynolds.

So I began work at ABC on December 7, 1970. At that time ABC had two serious problems with its evening news. It was getting about thirteen percent of the audience, as compared to twenty-five to thirty percent each for NBC and CBS. And even worse, it was being broadcast at only about 135 of the network's 200-odd affiliated stations. We had a first-class staff, we had enthusiasm, but we didn't have the stations.

I beg to brag a moment. Howard and I worked together well from the very start—he in Washington and me in New York—and we began to build an audience. There was a key moment that spring at the convention of affiliates in Los Angeles. I was given a chance to speak briefly to them, and since nobody had told me to be tactful, I wasn't. In the perilous days we were going through, I said, with the economy in trouble, with our youth progressively more alienated, with the war dragging on in Vietnam, with America's traditional values under question if not contempt, I thought that any network affiliate which did not carry that network's evening news was a disgrace to the broadcast industry.

Then we gave a cocktail party for all the stations that didn't carry us. We weren't sure anyone would show up, but they did, and in the following weeks, more importantly, they signed up. We had them all by the end of the year.

And with the new stations the rating went up. We peaked in 1973, with a highly respectable twenty-three- or twenty-four-percent share of the audience, with a solid and fast-footed program, with more and more attention to the show and to Howard's and my commentaries.

The program in those years was run by a kind of troika —Av Westin, Dick Richter, and Dave Buksbaum. They were all alumni of CBS, and I had worked with them all. They were—and are—highly talented. Buksbaum is the best operations executive—the guy who makes things happen—that I have ever known. He—like Palmer Williams and Phil Scheffler at *60 Minutes*—is a "Yes" man; that is, his inclination when you ask him if something can be done is to say, "Yes." You'd be surprised at how many executives have the opposite inclination. Or maybe you wouldn't; I suppose most businesses, from Mother Church to the local title-insurance company, have the same problem.

I don't want to go into great detail about the years at ABC. The first four years were so great that the gradual decline and disillusion of the last three still leave me feeling a little bruised and a bit incapable of an objective account. The bruising is complicated by a strong suspicion that it is something management and I collaborated on: we worked smoothly together to destroy an extremely promising operation. It hurt a number of people besides me—Buksbaum, for instance. And it didn't do Barbara Walters any good. Who were the villains? No villains, I think, just temporary dummies. If I, Bill Sheehan, and Fred Pierce were ever taken out together to be crucified for spoiling things, I honestly don't know who should get the cross in the center.

Okay, I'll do it briefly. We were doing so well in the first years that I think I got a little cocky, and a little lazier than usual. I have said at another point that I didn't take one kind of star role all that well, and that was probably true of the anchor role, too.

Anchoring is a funny talent. It works differently for different people. It worked for Howard and me, I think, because he had so many years of credibility and I don't think very many people thought I would lie to or try to manipulate them. But it is a grinding job, and it takes a daily, meticulous devotion. Maybe I didn't give it that. Maybe when Elmer Lower retired and Bill Sheehan took over, we lost a great ability—one of the greatest abilities a news executive can have—to deal with the executives of the entertainment side of the network. Maybe it was a wrong decision to let me go as a single anchor in the fall of 1975, with Howard just doing commentary; maybe I didn't work at it right. Certainly I was tired of anchoring; *60 Minutes* is more to my taste.

In any event, what happened is that we did go to a single anchor. We didn't do all that badly; after we reached a plateau and lost our momentum, we never dropped back to previous levels, and—discounting the added audiences ABC acquired by buying better affiliates in the years since I left— they've never done as well as we did in 1973. But there was the loss of something, and some of it was my fault. I don't know; I've got some explanations—explanations, not excuses or alibis. I'd explain some of it in terms of less than brilliant management. But I'd also explain some of it in terms of a period of soul-searching on my own, at home and at work, a period when I did not, as you have to do, put that damned daily show almost first in your life. I may have been going through some kind of mid-life crisis (I sometimes think I have been since just before my thirtieth birthday). We were never bad. But we lost a kind of verve and excitement.

And this offered an opportunity for a dangerous thing: it started Frederick Pierce thinking. Pierce had been around awhile, and then presided over an extraordinary rise in the fortunes of ABC's entertainment division. This gave him time to think about the news division, and he came up with the idea of the first male-female anchor team for a network news show, with Barbara Walters, of NBC's *Today Show*, as the female.

I resisted, and then gave in—chiefly because I thought that if I blocked that idea, it would be replaced with something worse. It was a bad idea—not because a woman co-anchor is a bad idea, not because Barbara Walters was a bad idea as an individual. It was a bad idea because, whether it was a stunt or not, it was going to be perceived as a stunt. It became a phenomenon we have seen elsewhere in the broadcast-news business: it attracted incredible attention from newspapers and magazines—cover stories, speculations on jealousies and chauvinism (both male and female), all that stuff. It attracted everything except an audience.

I don't think Barbara and I made a very good anchor team; I don't think her talent is in anchoring. But that was sort of irrelevant. It just could not have worked because of the perception—not the reality, the perception—of what people thought ABC was doing. It didn't work; we didn't even work together very long. But it sure made an impression. It took me two years back at *60 Minutes* before, in a public appearance, the first or second question would not be: "What was Barbara Walters really like?"

I suspect Barbara didn't like it any better than I did. I have said, struggling for syntax, that I think Barbara and I were the least of each other's problems, and I'd guess she would agree. I like Barbara Walters and admire her talents —which, as noted, I don't think include anchoring. She is— among other things, which include her own incredible ability to keep in touch with the press and with the stylish and famous—the victim of the vestiges of sexism. Mike Wallace does something outrageous and people call him brilliantly aggressive; Barbara does something similar and people call her bitchy. Cronkite stands windblown by a gantry at Cape Canaveral and people say he inspires confidence on the scene that way; Barbara does an on-the-scene interview in difficult circumstances looking something less than right out of a bandbox and people say the poor dear must have forgotten her hairdresser.

There are some advantages, also vestigial, in being a charming woman in this business. But they are probably outnumbered by what's left of people's attitudes on what a woman should be like and how she should behave.

May I say in defense of my own sex that I think these attitudes are at least as prevalent among women in the audience as they are among men?

Anyhow, Barbara will be all right. But the debacle of the two of us as a team led to a general shake-up. It led me to exercise my option of leaving—leaving, as a matter of candor, for nothing else in particular. I had made some money and for the first time in my life thought I could take six months off and brood about the meaning of life. It led to Bill Sheehan's departure and to the naming of Roone Arledge as president of ABC News. It led to what became known as the Arledge shell game, in which, by means of multiple anchors and other cosmetic devices, he more or less successfully concealed from the watching public the fact that Barbara was no longer any kind of an anchor.

As with the situation with Barbara, I have no case against Roone. He was brought in to salvage the wreckage of Fred Pierce's judgment, and he handled that challenge aggressively and with some success. He never offered me anything in particular, but, on the other hand, at our first meeting I told him I was firmly committed to leaving ABC on June 1, 1978. Our only arguments from then on were whether I was legally entitled to leave. By the time I was actually authorized to leave, it was known I was returning to CBS to replace Bill Moyers as the host on the *CBS Reports* documentaries. Roone believed for a time that it was all a conspiracy, that it had been arranged all along for me to go back to *60 Minutes*. Not so, Roone. *60 Minutes* was not even mentioned until I was back and working on two projects for *CBS Reports*, and there was some argument even then about whether it was a good idea.

So, seven and a half years after I first said "Good evening" for the *ABC Evening News*, I said it for the last time. I stayed on for a week, and this was the first hint to me that I had satisfied my ambition to be an anchorman. Someone came by around five o'clock on the first day I was in the office but not on camera and said: "Would you like a drink?"

I had a flooding sense of freedom. Most of the world begins to relax at the same time an anchorman begins to crank himself up. He is always introducing reports from interesting places he won't have a chance to see. He has to settle for money and prestige and, if he's any good, a sense of responsibility. There's nothing wrong with any of those things, but you can get most of them on *60 Minutes*, and I like it better.

There was one thing about the *ABC Evening News* that I don't have on *60 Minutes* and never had, really, as an anchor at CBS, and it was wonderful, and I'd like to talk about it, and demonstrate it, for a little while. It was the commentaries that closed the program and had been in use for some years before I joined. I was a little ambivalent about them, a little questioning that the audience could accept a reporter putting on a different hat and having opinions. It turned out they could. I was doubtful because I had always seen editorials as a function of management, of ownership, and I didn't know if commentaries were different enough to be acceptable. They were. I miss doing them, and I'd like to append a few of mine.

PANTYHOSE FOR MEN?

I don't want to get a reputation as an old fogey: I have enough problems already. I accept double-knit suits and loudly patterned shirts, and when a friend—male—showed up at the office today in black pumps with a red chain instead of laces, I said scarcely a word. I can even see where one of those electronic combs that blow hot air on your head while you are completing your morning comb-and-set might be fun. I'm in favor of people smelling better, so the increase in use of colognes and shower oils by men doesn't scare me. But I think there is a limit, and I think maybe Lord & Taylor, an otherwise respectable New York store, has reached it. They are offering, for the Christmas trade, pantyhose for men. Pantyhose for women are bad enough, but this is ridiculous. Lord & Taylor's version looks sort of like a pair of shorts attached to part of an old set of army winter underwear, in turn linked to a pair of support hose. To give the article what I suppose they think of as the Now look, they've got a sort of rally stripe leading down from the navel, like a Volkswagen pretending to be a Porsche. I know what the men's-liberation people will say—that they are sick and tired of fooling around with girdles and garter belts and runs in their nylons—but I still say that a man who can't keep up his socks without hooking them on his pelvis is going to be in trouble out in the real competitive world. It isn't as if we needed long underwear any more; most of us are not up at four to do the chores in the cold barn. Also, I suspect men may be physically at a disadvantage in pantyhose. There is, I've heard, a kind of swift, slick, wriggling maneuver required to get into them, that at one point means you have no feet at all on the floor; women can perform this maneuver and men can't. They would need a helper, or some kind of mechanical device, to lift them up from behind while they put on their underwear, which would add time and confusion to mornings. I appeal to my fellow men. Paint a racing stripe on your jockey shorts if you want to, but stay out of pantyhose.

Coming Apart

PANTYHOSE FOR MEN? A POSTSCRIPT

As a result of my remarks on Tuesday about men's panty-hose, I have received in the mail a pair of them from a manufacturer, which I guess qualifies as a normal business amenity rather than payola as long as I disclose it. The manufacturer suggests that I road-test them to be convinced that they are a practical garment and not a funky style. He says that his market research indicates the typical wearer of male pantyhose is about my age, about my style in dress —in a nutshell, he says, "the man who wears our Warm Johns might well be Harry Reasoner." I sort of resent that, but I guess I've got it coming. He further explains that the pantyhose were designed to combat an evil of the new fad of knit slacks and suit pants—a drawback he calls blow-through.

Anyhow, the above is something of a digression. What has fascinated me since Tuesday is the response to the piece. In this commentating racket, you put out what you sincerely hope is a reasoned, instructive, thoughtful piece on the Middle East or Pakistan or Red China or the international monetary crisis, and it frequently is like tossing a rock into a deep pond. Then you have a personal reaction to some vagary of life and it gets reprinted and people ask for copies and underwear manufacturers send you presents.

The easy conclusion to draw would be that people are shallow, more interested in their own underwear than in the future of what we laughingly call civilized man. But that's not necessarily so. I think they've learned from experience that weighty analyses of great and remote tragedies and confrontations don't always tell them anything new: it's up to journalism not only to learn more but to say more. And even more than that, I think people—Americans especially—have trouble dealing with something they can't do anything immediate about. They'll act to give money or to vote for something or even to go to war. But they have an understandable reluctance to brood about something they can't change.

Pantyhose, on the other hand, they can change.

THE NIXON PARDON

In the complex and distressing case of Richard Nixon, I guess I have to go along with President Ford.

There are two elements of confusion in the decision to pardon Mr. Nixon. One is the question of whether the pardon is basically a compassionate favor to the man or a political decision for the nation. I judge by reading Mr. Ford's statement it is mostly the latter, and that is proper. The second is how you view the disgrace of being the only man in history forced out of the presidency; if you don't see that as very strong punishment indeed, the pardon of course seems unjustified.

I suggest that this country is not used to or comfortable with political pardons, just as until the Nixon administration it was not used to political crimes in the White House. But in the case of political pardons the aim is to benefit the polity, not the criminal. I hope we don't have to get used to or comfortable with them, but in this case I think it is defensible.

However, much of the resentment of it is justified and understandable. Couldn't Mr. Ford defuse the anger and sense of wrong that so many people feel by extending, on a one-time basis, the pardon to everyone who is charged with essentially political crimes? I have been opposed to amnesty for draft-evaders and deserters, but perhaps now is the time to wipe out all those scores, without conditions, along with trying to write "The End" to Watergate.

And if Mr. Ford wants to end Watergate for the small fry and big enchiladas now in jail or awaiting trial, as today's news indicates, a more general amnesty for all the casualties of the travail of the last decade might be almost essential.

Of course, a blanket pardon for Watergate offenders, draft-evaders, and deserters would mean that a great many persons would get amnesty who clearly don't deserve it. But the precedent for that risk was established last Sunday.

13

Coming Back

I HAVE TO SAY that in the last years at ABC—say 1976—I felt pretty bad. I was wallowing in a lot of money and not enough self-respect. Whatever it was I had done so well for television, I wasn't doing it that well. As noted, I had contributed to the derailment of an ABC News organization of great promise.

I had, concomitantly, I think, not correlatively, blown a thirty-year marriage. This is not a book about marriage, and not in any great detail about my personal life, which, to use an old phrase from James Thurber, sometimes has seemed to resemble a dog's breakfast. But I mentioned Kay early on in the book and shouldn't just leave her there. Nothing I could write would meet her approval. Whenever you see a man in his fifties decide to leave a long-time wife, you can hardly be wrong in your judgment of him and your pity or contempt for him. Probably typically, I think it's not quite that way; I had thought for some years that we couldn't be worse apart and both of us might be better. In the face of that undocumented assertion you are entitled to think, and maybe rightly, that I was just another middle-aged fool. A lot of people thought that, including, part of the time, me.

Somebody entitled to ask me asked me: if there had been that much hidden tension in an outwardly ideal marriage, what had we gotten out of it to make it last that long? Twenty-eight years of passion, I said. Most men don't get that with any number of women. I *know* that; I'd be guessing if I said I don't think most women do either. I think I made it clear that, compared to a lot of hot dogs I know, I have not been intimate with a lot of women. But I have known an incredibly classy group. And in a lot of the ways that make men and women important to each other, Kay stood alone.

So THERE I was, wallowing, when Bill Small asked me, during the Christmas season of 1977, if when I left ABC I would like to return to CBS. I had not really thought of that as a possibility until the previous spring, when Kay and I had gone to see the Kentucky Derby as guests of Barry Bingham, Junior, and his wife. The Binghams run the *Louisville Courier-Journal* and the CBS affiliate in Louisville, and every year they invite two CBS couples down to stay with them and go to all those Derby parties and drink all that good whiskey. I think this year they invited the Smalls and the Reasoners because Barry wanted me to come back. I think so, and I'm flattered.

Small had been my boss in Washington; he was at Derby time vice president in charge of hard news and the assumed eventual successor to Dick Salant as president. What happened there I don't know; Bill Leonard got the job instead and Small went over to be president of NBC News. I don't know the plot; I know a lot of people have found Bill hard to understand. All I know is he has always been straight and fair with me and he took the trouble to get me back. So before that Christmas lunch when he issued a formal invitation, we sat in May in the mosquitoey and muggy Kentucky night and agreed that if the right opportunity ever came up, I'd like to come back.

Incidentally, Seattle Slew won that day. Altogether I made about $65, and the Binghams bought the drinks.

I HAD TOLD BILL I'd like to come back, but there were a lot of interior reservations. I had gotten, as well as depressed and unwarrantedly and unhelpfully introspective, a little fat and soft on a lot of money. I knew that anything CBS wanted me for would mean a lot less money and a return to playing reporter instead of pampered anchor; I was sick at where I stood, but not terribly confident that I could do what I used to do.

The difference there, the element that gave me the guts to go back, was a woman I met in December 1974. You are saying, "A-ha! There is the explanation of the marriage break-up, the final piece in the puzzle." I don't think so, but those of you who are saying a-ha are in the majority.

Anyhow, during the four years that we knew each other, uncommitted but loving, she rebuilt my professional ego. Nobody else of her sex with even greater access to that ego (you can guess who I mean) seemed much interested in that. So she made it seem right and fine and a good bet to take a cut in pay and go back to work and see if I still had the legs. That was during the casual four years; in the ensuing time when we became committed, things got a lot tougher, but that's life, too.

So in the summer of 1978 I went back to CBS News. I had left loving almost everyone, from executives to the important people like cameramen and Hewitt, and it was easy. It was, I think, a mild summer, and after two weeks of between networks (I had planned on six months, you may remember) I checked in. I had two determinations: not to blow the job this time, and not to capriciously lose the woman who had made it feasible, if Bill Small made it possible.

Both determinations have been varyingly iffy since. But I don't think I'll blow the job. I came back a lot calmer, a lot easier in relations with my colleagues. Maybe, sometime in your fifties or sixties, even people like me begin to grow up.

The first on-the-air thing I did when I got back was to anchor a small afternoon special report—you know, the thing when they interrupt your soap opera with a little sign that says "CBS News Special Report." This was to show by satellite the moving of the body of Pope Paul from his summer place to the Vatican. The broadcast ended, and for the first time in seven and a half years I looked at the camera and said, "This is Harry Reasoner, CBS News."

The woman referred to above called a few minutes later. "Considering the story," she said, "you sounded inappropriately joyous."

Yes.

End-Piece

S O HERE WE ARE—spring of 1981 at this writing; new President in the White House, new face in the anchor chair of the *CBS Evening News*, new tensions in a world my generation cannot claim to have never made. Any final thought, Reasoner? You started out by talking about having been around during the precocious childhood, the aggressive youth and maturity, and—you said—perhaps the premature old age of television news. Fairly heavy premise. Have you justified it in these brief notes, or are you prepared to now?

No. I watched a young writer interviewed on television the other day who had just finished a book about the growth and, as I gathered was his judgment, the disintegration of a popular journal that came out of the turmoil of the sixties and then sort of joined the new establishment. He was trying to articulate the feelings and the sort of inchoate disappointment of people who are now in their thirties. We thought, he said, that we were really going to change things in a qualitative way. That we were going to change the way people got along with each other, that we were going to stop war and greed, and that we and our children were going to sit around peacefully smoking dope and loving each other and eating organically grown vegetables. We made some changes, but they were quantitative.

He made sense, too, but since I was watching the interview with a person of thirty-two, I checked. "Oh, yes," was the reply, "we lost something, a spirit, a feeling that the dumb things we did would actually count."

"You found out," I suggested, "that we are all people. Imperfect by definition, and of limited attention span." A man I knew was once asked if he felt any threat from the young people who were charging out of the schools in the 1950's and joining the world's work force. He, and I, would have been perhaps thirty-two at the time. "No," he said, "I just think of them as rapidly becoming contemporaries."

We do, don't we? We are so bound up in our own emotional intestines that we very rapidly at any adult age have the same griping problems; we are so caught up in the things we have to do that we forget the nice parts—the mists and tides of love, the feel of rocks in a country driveway on a chilly spring day that have sat in the new sun until you pick a couple up and they are warmer than the air, the exhilaration of pure life. We seem to justify everything cynical Shakespeare ever said, and Mark Twain summing up his own late feeling: "the damned human race," he said.

But what about a couple of tidy conclusions about journalism, about broadcast journalism in particular? I think we've got some problems. As well as some triumphs. We now do routinely that which was experimental and hazardous to our corporate health; we do a better job than any *mass* journalism in the history of the world. And our problems reflect our society. Journalism is, after all, the current events of anthropology, and it might be more valuable to a future historian or anthropologist to see that the local television news of the 1980's was frequently silly than to know more of the serious events it did not report.

At the network level there is one problem that worries me, which is that we are too much the familiars of the people we report on. I remember as a very junior correspondent watching Ed Murrow on one of the first international programs. It was a Friendly idea in the time before satellites; what he did was set up an interviewee in London, say, with film crew and camera, and Murrow in New York with film crew and camera, and link the two with a telephone line for a conversation as both cameras rolled. The first one I saw involved Murrow talking to a famous British general of World War II.

"Let's begin this way, Pug," said Murrow. How in the world, I thought, can you ask a hard question of a man you know as Pug? It's worse now; too many of us interview the people we have had dinner with the night before. I think journalists and subjects can be mutually respectful friends, but when you are close enough so that you are no longer adversaries, our profession or craft or racket—craft, I think we decided—is in trouble. I very occasionally in a forgetful mood get trapped into a kind of New York dinner where there are beautiful people around, some of them very nice.

I did the other night, and the lady on my right asked, "Have you seen Henry since he got back in town?" I was about to say "Henry who?" when I remembered that this lady was notorious, to me at least, for a complete absence of humor, and of course I knew she meant the former Secretary of State, Mr. Kissinger, who had just concluded an embarrassing tour of some far reaches of the world. So I just said no, I didn't know Mr. Kissinger very well.

Knowing people, being on first-name terms or even privy to diminutives, has some advantages. But it is also very dangerous. Maybe we have been too successful, which is why we are, I'm afraid, a bit prematurely old. We have lost some strange and invigorating sense of being outsiders.

I remember a conversation I had some years ago with a relative, a geologist. We were talking about some endangered animal, the whispering curlew or the whooping crane or something, and I expressed the feeling that it would not survive. Of course not, he said. Everything in his scientific discipline taught him that nothing would survive: the United States would go, and man would go, and probably the universe would go or so change as to be uninteresting to those of us who loved it. It's a strangely comforting thought, I guess. You can live with a temporary rebuff if you think of CBS News in terms of an organization that will before long, geologically speaking, be not even a memory. But it is an idea repugnant to most journalists, and to most Americans.

Because along with the justified cynicism, and the justified feeling that everything seems to be going to hell, we retain our basic optimism, and some inside feeling that man as a whole and Americans in particular don't have to be like the whispering curlew. We ought to be able to make some sense out of what we're doing, and stop the worst of it, and limp along. We *have* made some progress both as journalists and as citizens in my lifetime: we won the war we had to win, for instance. And we have pretty well disposed of the idea that people should be limited in their choices of how to live and where and with whom because of their color or their reproductive facilities. We have on some precious occasions, like July 4, 1976, held each other's hands and said I love you.

Journalism cannot and should not foster this sort of thing; it should, however, report it. It should be human without being maudlin, aware of sentiment while shying from sentimentalism. It should be awake.

In 1969, I think it was, I spent some time in Israel and chose to do my end-piece—the stand-upper—at the Allenby Bridge across the Jordan River. The young Israeli escort officer who had been my companion asked me what conclusions and recommendations I was going to voice. "None," I said, "I'm a reporter. I don't make recommendations." He was incredulous. "Your employer," he said, "sent you and the film crew here at unbelievable expense, we have given you every facility to prowl and poke and ask, and you have no conclusions? Shame on you."

I disagree with him, of course, but he had a point. Our reporting should not be exhortative or evangelistic, but it should be sharp enough so that things can be learned from it.

After all, reporting is just another human activity,

another form of work. And many years ago Kay Reasoner told me the Catholic theological definition of "work." It is hard to forget, and means more to me every year I fail to live up to so many standards.

"Work," said the theologian, "is the effort of men and women to bring order out of the chaos left by original sin."

As you may have noticed, there is no shortage of chaos around.

Some people believe it is redundant for me to say I could not have done this book without Jean Dudasik Roy, because they don't think I can do anything without Jean Dudasik Roy. Some truth in that. We have been together for something like thirteen years, establishing a record for mutual tolerance.

There are an awful lot of other people whose names don't get in the book that have been essential to what I've been doing the last twenty-five years—cameramen, writers, Frances Arvold, editors, technicians, producers, salesmen, all kinds of people, even including some executives. They are the people who made it mostly fun. They know who they are.

ABOUT THE AUTHOR

Harry Reasoner was born in 1923 in Dakota City, Iowa, and educated at Stanford University and the University of Minnesota. He began work as a journalist on the Minneapolis *Times* in 1942, and after military service in World War II returned to the *Times* as drama critic. He spent three years with the USIA in Manila and started in television in 1954, coming to CBS in 1956. Except for eight years (1970–1978) at ABC, he has been with CBS ever since. He is currently one of four co-editors on the top-rated CBS program *60 Minutes*, which he originally helped to launch in 1968. Reasoner is the author of a novel, *Tell Me About Women,* and of a collection of broadcast pieces entitled *The Reasoner Report.*

A NOTE ON THE TYPE

This book was set on the Linotype in Granjon, a type named in compliment to Robert Granjon, but neither a copy of a classic face nor an entirely original creation. George W. Jones based his designs on the type used by Claude Garamond (1510–61) in his beautiful French books. Granjon more closely resembles Garamond's own type than do any of the various modern types that bear his name.

Robert Granjon began his career as type cutter in 1523. The boldest and most original designer of his time, he was one of the first to practice the trade of type founder apart from that of printer. Between 1557 and 1562 Granjon printed about twenty books in types designed by himself, following, after the fashion, the cursive handwriting of the time. These types, usually known as caractères de civilité, he himself called lettres françaises, as especially appropriate to his own country.

This book was composed by Maryland Linotype Composition Co., Inc., Baltimore, Maryland, and printed and bound by American Book-Stratford Press, Inc., Saddle Brook, New Jersey.

Typography and binding design by
VIRGINIA TAN